Love Virtue

OTHER BOOKS BY CARL JAPIKSE:

The Light Within Us
Poems of Light
The Hour Glass
Exploring the Tarot
The Tarot Journal
The Enlightened Management Journal
The $1.98 Cookbook
The Biggest Tax Cheat in America is the I.R.S.

as Waldo Japussy:

The Tao of Meow
The Ruby Cat

with Robert R. Leichtman, M.D.:

Active Meditation
Forces of the Zodiac
The Light of Learning
Tapping Our Rich Potential
Perfecting the Emotions
Harnessing Our Noble Mind
Expanding Our Horizons
Completing the Masterpiece
The Life of Spirit
Our Spiritual Resources
The Divine Workshop
Healing Lines
Ruling Lines
Connecting Lines
Changing Lines

LOVE VIRTUE

by Carl Japikse

ARIEL PRESS
Atlanta, Georgia & Columbus, Ohio

No royalties are paid on this book

This book is made possible
by a gift to the Publications Fund of Light
from Judith Renaud Ross

LOVE VIRTUE
Copyright © 2000 by Light

All Rights Reserved. No part of this book may be used or reproduced in any manner without written permission, except in the case of brief quotations embodied in articles and reviews. Printed in the United States of America. Direct inquiries to: Ariel Press, P.O. Box 297, Marble Hill, GA 30148.

ISBN 0-89804-087-6

Table of Contents

The Loss of Virtue	8
Absolute Truth	16
The Essence of All Things	22
Irresistible to Mankind	27
A Source of Strength	35
Stealing from Angels	42
Split in Halves	46
Vice—Or Virtue?	56
Taking Charge	60
Twelve Key Virtues	67
Goodwill	69
Wisdom	72
Generosity	76
Courage	79
Cheerfulness	82
Reverence	85
Harmony	88
Justness	92
Temperance	96
Integrity	100
Beauty	104
Patience	107
Integrating Virtue	110
A Call for Virtue	114
Contacting Virtue	120
Teaching Virtue to Children	124
Restoring Virtue in Society	131
The Legacy of Virtue	135
A Person of Virtue	137
A Collect on Virtue	139
Recommended Reading	142

Editor's Note:

Translations of scriptures quoted
in this book are
by the author.

Love
Virtue

*"Happy the man who meditates on wisdom,
and reasons with good sense,
who studies her ways in her heart,
and ponders on her secrets."*
—Ecclesiasticus, 14:20-21

The Loss of Virtue

One hundred and fifty years ago, in the days of Emerson, Harriet Beecher Stowe, and Abraham Lincoln, America was proud to be a land of virtue. A virtuous character was extolled as a great achievement; virtue was a driving force that impelled lethargic humanity to scale the heights, be they Everest or spiritual perfection. It was assumed that every thinking person would want to behave with virtue.

Indeed, the whole fabric of our American society, starting with the Declaration of Independence and the Constitution, is woven from this assumption. It forms the basis of Thomas Jefferson's proclamation of "an inalienable right to life, liberty, and the pursuit of happiness." A few years later, in writing *Common Sense,* Thomas Paine argued eloquently that the only reason society even needs government is because some individual human beings lack sufficient virtue to govern themselves. As the level of virtue throughout a society increases and deepens, the need of that society to depend upon the "necessary evil" of government decreases.

The role of "virtue" in human living remained deeply embedded in the thoughts and assumptions of thinking Americans throughout the eighteenth and nineteenth centuries. But today, at the cusp of a new millenium, the idea of virtue has fallen from its pedestal. We no longer regard virtue as a necessary ideal for human living—or even something fashionable. If one dares mention the word in a public lecture, one is apt to be told in no uncertain terms that "sophisticated people" no longer consider virtue to be a necessary part of human living. Virtue, it seems, has lost its relevance.

The current whims of "sophisticated people" are of little importance. They are the modern descendants of the ancient Greek *sophists*—a group of traveling demagogues who believed only in the art of persuasion, not in truth. While Socrates and Plato were busy teaching their students that the object of thinking was to understand themselves and life, the sophists were occupied teaching their followers that the purpose of thinking was to win arguments and gain power over others. Sophisticated people, in other words, have never been guardians of virtue.

It is troubling, however, that virtue is perceived by many as irrelevant in modern society. Too many people have turned away from virtue, and we are beginning to feel the impact in our national character. We are on the verge of losing the strength that has always characterized America—and is the heart of virtue.

This loss of virtue has been occurring steadily for the past seventy-five years. The effort of the Prohibitionists to impose their idea of "virtue" on the rest of the country certainly symbolizes the inauguration of the modern, anti-virtue era. In this act, and others since, the noble idea of virtue has become identified with moral righteousness and, even worse, the desire to impose one chosen set of values on the whole country. Such crusades as McCarthyism and others have led many people to associate virtue exclusively with religious fanaticism. The thought that the virtue of Thomas Paine and Ralph Waldo Emerson could be reduced to the ravings of religious zealots is appalling, but nonetheless one that is widely accepted in America today.

The signs of the decline of virtue as a governing ideal in American life are found throughout our society:

- The Presidency has been degraded by a man with so little moral strength that he openly embraced oral sex in the Oval Office, then lied repeatedly about it to the American public, both in and out of the courts.
- Discipline has disappeared from our nation's schools. Teachers are afraid of restraining children, lest they be sued. As a result, children bring weapons to schools with impunity and open fire on their classmates, in order to get attention.
- Librarians are afraid of asking loud-mouthed

individuals to keep quiet out of respect for other readers, lest they be fired for "interfering with the individual's library experience."

- We sue one another whenever we are in any way inconvenienced. As a whole, we take almost no responsibility for maintaining our own health, educating ourselves, or providing for our own well-being. It is always someone else's fault—and financial responsibility.
- The media has lost its way in a sea of ambiguity. Fifty years ago, journalists at least paid lip service to the ideal of objectivity in their stories and reports. Today, they actively sneer at objectivity, and believe that the only useful report is one which has been colored by their own opinions—without warning the unsuspecting public, of course. Sophism lives.
- A sizeable portion of the American public openly endorses the unrestricted use of recreational drugs, which are readily available. Although massive campaigns have been launched to educate the public about the dangers of using drugs, little progress is being made—primarily because the public will to eradicate drug usage has not been tapped.
- Public debate on major issues is conducted primarily by confrontation, thereby polarizing any discussion. Instead of searching for options or al-

ternatives that most people could agree on—the method used to shape the Constitution—policy advocates now regularly demonize their opponents and reduce debate to blatant misrepresentation of legitimate perspectives.

- It has been adjudged "politically incorrect" to voice opposition to a number of select issues, ranging from homosexuality to abortion rights.
- Jack Kervorkian was allowed to commit a score of murders before he was convicted and sentenced for an assisted suicide.
- A person can be fired from political office after he correctly uses the word "niggardly," because it is misinterpreted by poorly-educated blacks as a racial slur.

Each of these examples—and there are thousands more of the same—represents a conflict between the "Prohibitionaries" and the "Permissionaries" in our society. The Prohibitionaries are the direct descendents of the Temperance movement. They believe that naughty behavior can best be controlled by outlawing it. They therefore want government to restrict everything they disdain—homosexuality, abortion, drugs, and much more. Lately, they have been joined by a new group of Prohibitionaries— people who advocate banning the use of tobacco. Lining up in the wings are other groups salivating at the prospect of issuing other bans—against the consumption of meat, the wearing of furs, and the productive use of our lands or resources.

The Permissionaries are those who see such bans as threatening and undemocratic—but then take their opposition to Prohibitionism to the polar extreme. Instead of advocating tolerance and goodwill for all people, they have adopted an "in your face" militancy designed to impose unpopular lifestyles on our education, military, culture, and society. These people will not rest until the Declaration of Independence has been rewritten so that it says "Anything Goes" instead of Jefferson's famous line, "life, liberty, and the pursuit of happiness."

The unfortunate victim of this cultural clash between the Prohibitionaries and Permissionaries has been the ideal of virtue. All too often, the Prohibitionaries have hidden behind the shield of virtue, insisting on their moral high ground. But there is no moral high ground in classifying and treating whole groups of people as either outlaws or inferior citizens just because their lifestyle varies from our own. As a result, the value of virtue has been demeaned by the very people who claim to love it, through their indecent intolerance of their fellow citizens.

At the same time, however, even more blame for the destruction of virtue falls at the feet of the Permissionaries, who view virtue as a kind of hobgoblin of the holier-than-thou-crowd. In trying to correct an injustice in society, they have grossly overreacted. The result has been to throw out virtue as well as intolerance and prejudice.

And yet, as unfortunate as this development is, it is clearly not the end of virtue. Humanity does not have the option to kill or even seriously damage virtue, because virtue is not of human origin. Virtue is a gift to us from divine life, a kind of grace that is added to us as we learn to invest it in all that we do. We can spurn virtue and deny it, but we cannot eradicate it.

Indeed, virtue is still as important to our society and our happiness as individuals as it was two thousand years ago and two hundred years ago. Even though we as a people have become estranged from the meaning and experience of virtue, it is our loss, not virtue's. It is our lives and our understanding that suffer. It is therefore important to see the need to restore virtue to its proper eminence in our culture and thinking—but cleansed and purified of its unholy baggage.

Virtue is one of the great keys to living a sane, well-contented life. It helps us aspire to the best within us, and learn to express it in our daily activities. In times of challenge, it is virtue that provides us with the strength to endure and triumph. In times of depression, it is virtue that empowers us to rise out of our ruts and discover the transcendent dimensions of life. In times of sickness, it is virtue that enables the great healing force of life to work within us.

The ancients knew the value of virtue, and based their whole approach to life upon it. The usefulness of virtue was reborn again at the beginning of the Renaissance, and honored during the Age of Enlightenment. It has only been in our modern Age of Doubt that virtue has lost its prominence.

The purpose of this book is to reawaken us to the value of virtue, and describe how to reclaim it as a vital presence in our lives. To do this, however, we must first learn what virtue is, and then we must make it a central part of our daily lives.

We must learn to love virtue.

Absolute Truth

The indispensable role that virtue plays in human living has been known for thousands of years, and can be found in every major culture throughout the globe—in ancient Greece, Rome, China, India, the Middle East, and Europe.

In Greece, virtue was referred to as "arete," which emphasizes the element of excellence—striving for the best within us. Socrates taught that *arete* was the inner essence of knowledge, the wisdom to use any Idea properly.

To grasp this definition of virtue fully, it is important to realize that Socrates (and Plato after him) held that there are two kinds of ideas—concrete ideas, such as the laws of a city, and abstract Ideas, such as Justice. While concrete ideas, like laws, can be changed, and even applied unevenly to different people, abstract ideas, like Justice, are universal and unchangeable. They are absolute.

For Socrates, therefore, "virtue" did not mean just moral perfection—a definition which was introduced two generations later by Aristotle. It described, instead, the ability to interact directly with abstract principles such as Justice, Harmony, Beauty, Goodwill, and Wisdom. Virtue was the essence of thought that "abides in the real, eternal absolute," as opposed to our concepts of it.

Socrates also stated that these inner, abstract principles could be contacted and known only through the development of the rational mind. This is done by filling our thoughts with known abstract principles—Harmony, Beauty, Truth, and so on. As the mind extends itself in this way, it becomes filled with virtue, the dynamic link that connects us with the absolute.

It was the life-long goal of Socrates to explore as much of these realms of the eternal absolute as he could. He would proudly announce that he was the most ignorant man in Athens, not because he knew less than anyone else, but rather because he knew that he was ill-informed about the absolute—and most of his fellow country-men did not even know enough about it to recognize that they were ill-informed! This aspect of human life remains largely unchanged today.

Xenophon, a student of the great Socrates, illustrated the importance of virtue in a story about the mythological hero, Heracles (in Rome, he was known as Hercules). According to Xenophon, Heracles was confronted, while still a lad, by the demigods Virtue and Pleasure. The two gods demanded that Heracles choose between them. Pleasure offered him temporal power and complete physical satisfaction; Virtue promised him only immortality. Heracles chose Virtue over Pleasure.

He spent his human life as a great hero, conquering foe after foe, both human and divine. He suffered tremendously, and was forced to perform twelve seemingly impossible labors. When his labors were completed, though, he was elevated to the status of god and granted immortality.

In this brief story, an important part of virtue is illustrated. The pursuit of pleasure and desire traps us in the darkened prison of materialism, leading to suffering and torment. The pursuit of virtue liberates us from the prison, and sets us on a path that leads eventually to a recognition of our innate immortality—not the immortality of the physical form, which dies, but the immortality of the inner part of us, the part that was created in God's image, as recounted in the book of Genesis.

The offspring of a human mother and a divine father (Zeus), Heracles is the perfect role model for virtue. He is a link between heaven and earth, capable of summoning superhuman abilities of strength, courage, wisdom, and bravery through his virtue. Assigned impossible tasks, he nonetheless faces them with undaunting fortitude—and triumphs.

Plato, who had likewise studied with Socrates, took his teacher's ideas about *arete* and expanded upon them throughout his writings. Among other things, he expostulated four cardinal virtues that link the human being to the absolute, both in our thinking and our behavior:

- Wisdom, the ability to understand the puzzles of life and heal inner conflicts.
- Courage, the strength of heart that motivates us to excel.
- Temperance, the capacity to exercise self-control and discipline.
- Justice, the ability to act in accord with the highest design, and to restore balance whenever this design has been violated.

To Plato, these virtues had a transcendent, absolute power. When contacted by a thoughtful person, each of these qualities would bring with it the power to reorganize his or her thinking, values, and understanding. Virtue was the only power that could accomplish this. Mere experience lacked this power. The observation of others likewise lacked this power. The established laws of a government lacked this power. Only virtue possessed it. To Plato, this was why virtue was the one indispensable quality of the perfected human being.

Hundreds of years after the death of Plato, his concept of four cardinal virtues was revived by Plotinus, at the onset of the neo-Platonic movement in the early Christian church. In order to make his teachings more compatible with Christian tradition, however, the famous trilogy of virtues enunciated by St. Paul in 1 Corinthians 13—faith, hope, and love—were added to Plato's original four. In this way, the seven cardinal virtues taught by the Catholic church were born.

As the glory of Greece began to wane, eclipsed by the emerging civilization of Rome, the Latin word "virtus" replaced the Greek word "arete." Virtus was derived from the Latin root *vir*, meaning "manliness" or "human potency." In popular usage, it also lost most of the original meaning embued by Socrates and Plato. It came to refer only to outward displays of great bravery and courage—or, in its Christian usage, morality.

The history of the word *virtue* is a good illustration of how certain words in our vocabulary can be degraded and robbed of their original potency. In its original sense, *virtue* had the meaning of "the power that can make all things new." Throughout the centuries, however, its primary meaning has been either forgotten or twisted into unrecognizable forms. Our use of the word "virtual" underscores this point. One would expect it to mean "of or containing virtue." In other words, a "virtual connection to God" would describe the most intimate link with the divine life possible. But "virtual" no longer retains this meaning! Today, it suggests an approximation, an illusion, or an imitation.

A virtual tornado would be a lesser storm that appears to be a tornado but is not. A virtual dictator might be a president that acts in dictatorial ways, although democratically elected. Virtual reality is the semblance of reality, rather than reality itself.

The same loss of vigor has occurred with our modern concepts of virtue. For most people, virtue is whatever they happen to define as the highest, noblest reaches of human behavior. It has nothing whatsoever to do with establishing a link with transcendent energies, as it did for Socrates and Plato.

The result? A loss of the inner power that virtue can bring into the life of the intelligent individual.

But this loss of virtue is not just a personal tragedy, affecting a few individuals. Far more important is the collective loss that has occurred as public opinion has turned against virtue. Society itself is being deprived of the inflow of this needed power. It is being left without the power it needs to steer its course through turbulent waters.

It is time to reverse this trend.

It is time to learn to love virtue.

The Essence of All Things

Virtue is not just an invention of Western philosophy, however. It plays a central role in every major culture that has developed on earth.

In India, for example, virtue is a key to understanding the original benevolent intent of the caste system, as opposed to the many corruptions which distorted it in practice. The Vedas, a set of writings in Sanskrit which correspond to the Mosaic laws of the Jewish tradition, taught that virtue is our primary connection to divine life. Through virtue, we are able to discover our perfect divine design for living. As we strive to express this perfect design through our work, relationships, and daily activities, we become known as a virtuous person. There is just one problem. Most human beings have not pursued the practice of union with God (yoga) sufficiently to be aware of this divine connection called virtue, let alone express it in daily living.

To compensate for this lack of understanding, the Vedas laid out a caste system. Each caste determined the kind of work the individual was to perform—warrior, ruler, priest, merchant, laborer, and so on. In this way, even an unenlightened person would know his purpose and duty in life, because it was dictated to him by his caste. While this system seems to the Western mind to be a denial of individual choice, it did not present any such conflict to the Eastern mind, which understood that the choice of caste was made prior to birth by the individual's soul. A rigid caste system therefore kept the personality from violating the intent of its soul. All the individual had to do was strive to excel in his or her particular caste.

Unfortunately, the caste system was distorted by human practice, as it became a tool for social stratification and discrimination. Nonetheless, we should not overlook the lesson behind it. As we assert our individuality and talent as a human being, we are meant to discover the virtue within us— and use it to establish a conscious awareness of our connection with divine life. We are likewise meant to assess the opportunities of our life and choose those that best reflect the noblest elements within us. This is the heart of virtue.

The dilemma of making these choices is brilliantly captured in the Hindu scripture, *The Bhagavad-Gita*, a part of the Vedas. The *Gita* tells the story of Arjuna and his conversation with Krishna, the incarnation of God, in the hours before the battle of Kurukshetra. Arjuna, a member of the warrior caste, is duty-bound to fight in the battle, but the war pits him against friends and relatives. He worries that he may have to kill someone he cares for, and this would be the worst evil he could imagine. Krishna tells him that his first duty is to God, and that God has appointed him to be a warrior. Virtue therefore demands that he be the best warrior he can, even if circumstance forces him to kill friends and relatives. He is not a servant of circumstance, but a servant of his innate divine design:

> If a man plays no part in the grand drama of life,
> His life becomes evil. He puts himself before God.
> Know this, Arjuna: his life counts for nothing.

Through this story, Krishna, the god within us, reminds Arjuna, the confused personality, that he was placed on earth to serve his inner, divine design—not to be driven by the winds of circumstance. Our connection to this inner, divine design is virtue.

The role of virtue in life was also nurtured in ancient China. One of the most important writings in the development of Chinese thought is the *Tao Te Ching*, written by Lao Tsu, a high-ranking government official who was forced out of office late in his life. As he journeyed back to his home province in retirement, he set down his reflections on public life and the wise use of power in 81 stanzas, *The Book of the Way to Virtue*. The word "te" is Chinese for virtue.

Lao Tsu defines the Tao as the manifested intelligence of the Absolute. While the Absolute is unchanging, being divine, the Tao is constantly in flux, as it is created of the *yang* and the *yin*, the masculine and the feminine. According to Lao Tsu, nothing on earth ever remains itself; it is always seeking to change into its opposite reflection. Winter turns into summer, just as spring turns into autumn.

In human life, this principle is profound. Ignorance forces us to become wise, as we confront the numerous mistakes we make. The interval between ignorance and wisdom may be enormous, but the very design of life forces us to overcome our deficit. Just so, the only way we can hold onto authority is to give it to others, thereby putting it to work.

The object of all of this experience is virtue. Lao Tsu holds out the image of "a man of virtue" as the highest possible attainment of human consciousness. As we read the text, it becomes clear that Lao Tsu was not just referring to a good and decent person in this regard. To Lao Tsu, virtue is the one element that links men and women to the Tao and allows us to act in harmony with it. As he puts it in verse 79:

> A man of virtue plays his role fully,
> While those who lack virtue rely on others
> to complete their tasks.

> The Tao courts no favorites.
> It grants the man of virtue immortality.

Even though the Tao is the manifest expression of the Absolute, and virtue is our link to it, Lao Tsu makes it clear that both the Tao and virtue are exceedingly subtle. They have no physical form. They cannot be poured into a bottle and sold on a "shelf of virtues" at a local health food store. Virtue is the essence of the best within us. It is invisible and immortal. As Lao Tsu states in verse 4:

> Virtue is the essence of all things,
> A fountain from which life springs.
> It is the courage to embrace sharpness,
> The wisdom to unravel complexities,
> The harmony that softens garishness,
> The abstract within the concrete.
> Deep, but as close as your heart!
> I do not know its origins,
> But it has always been found in great men.

Another great Chinese thinker, Confucius, likewise emphasized the central role of virtue in human development, stating that it is through virtue that we reclaim our divinity. He listed goodwill as the highest virtue, above all others, and then added reciprocity, loyalty, courage, wisdom, and trust.

Irresistible to Mankind

The greatest exposition of the role of virtue in human life lies, however, in the Hebrew and Christian scriptures. From the opening chapter of the book of Genesis, it is quite clear that there is a special connection between God and Man. God created mankind in His own image, by scooping together a handful of dust, focusing His creative intent, and then breathing life into the resulting shape. This passage is usually interpreted as describing the creation of human physical bodies, but in fact it refers to the creation of the human soul. As God breathed into the soul of all humanity, Adam, He imparted His own virtue, His own essence and will.

Within this story of Creation lies the key to the puzzle of human life. Because God animated the soul with His own virtue, the virtue which links us to Adam (the soul) is the path by which we can reclaim the garden of Eden. It is the most direct path, and in fact, the only path. By learning to express virtue in all that we do, we return to our rightful place in Paradise.

It needs to be understood that God did not create human beings one at a time. He created Adam, representing the sum of all human beings, and then He used a rib from Adam—part of his virtue—to create Eve, representing the sum of all human personalities. This passage in the Bible has no reference to human gender; it is an allegory depicting the relationship of the personality to the soul.

In the Hebraic tradition, therefore, virtue is literally the presence of God's life and spirit within humanity as a whole, and within each of us individually. As an individual, we are expected to act with virtue in all that we do. The same is expected of every race, ethnic group, and nation—in fact, of humanity as a whole. The fact that we fail to express virtue both individually and collectively does not in any way dilute the meaning or role of virtue in our lives. It simply underscores the poignancy of our ignorance.

When developed and expressed, it is virtue that links us to spirit; it is virtue that connects us with God. To put it in grander terms, virtue is the bolt of energy transmitted by God to Adam in the grand fresco by Michaelangelo on the ceiling of the Sistine Chapel; it is the animation of life on earth as depicted by William Blake in his painting of the Ancient of Days. Virtue is not the same as the soul; it is, instead, our connection to the soul. It is our birthright as sons and daughters of God. It embraces and preserves our reason for being here on earth.

One of the most complete expositions of virtue in the Judeo-Christian tradition is the book of Wisdom, also known as "The Wisdom of Solomon," although it is unlikely it was written by Solomon. It has always been part of the Catholic Bible, but was dropped by many of the Protestant sects in the seventeenth century. It was part of the original King James Version—and has been included once again in the recent Jerusalem Bible.

On the surface, the book of Wisdom appears to be a treatise on the principles of good government, similar in purpose to *The Tao Te Ching* or *The Republic* by Plato. In fact, however, it is a clear statement of the value of self-government in general and virtue in specific. According to Solomon, a proper life begins with virtue. In fact, the book opens with the exhortation:

> Love virtue!
> Let open-mindedness direct your thinking
>   to the Lord;
> Seek God in the simplicity of your heart.
> Do not try to prove or disprove God:
> He reveals Himself only to those who trust Him.
> The selfish divorce themselves from God,
>   The attempt to test God bewilders the foolish.

This opening salvo states the value of virtue clearly. In order to acquire wisdom, we must first learn to love and express virtue. The foolish person who demands proof of God's existence is exactly what he advertises—a fool. The only proof of God anyone needs is the discovery of our connection with God, deep within us—virtue. The opposite of virtue, all forms of selfishness, is the trap that alienates us from a full relationship with the divine.

Solomon continues (2:23 to 3:1):

> God made Adam in His own image;
> The soul of man cannot perish.
> Even though the personality dies,
> The souls of the virtuous are in the hands of God;
> No suffering can mislead them.

Being a gift of spirit, virtue does not help us attain immortality. *Virtue is already and always has been immortal.* To the degree that we discover and express the virtue deep within us, we identify with the immortal octaves of our being. We reverse our views of the meaning of death and suffering.

Solomon's main interest, of course, is not with virtue; his text deals with wisdom. But he knows that most human beings confuse wisdom for opinion. So he wants to make it clear that genuine wisdom comes from divine life, not from human opinion or convention. What we believe, in fact, is far more likely to estrange us from God than bring us nearer to Him.

To address this difficulty, Solomon makes it clear that it is the virtue within wisdom—the will inherent in God's blueprints for human expression—that characterizes wisdom, not our willingness to believe. Without virtue, wisdom—or beauty or goodwill or honor or temperance—is just a hollow vessel. The only true wisdom, in other words, is that which links us to divine comprehension. Solomon spells it out in more detail in chapter 7:

> Within wisdom there is a spirit.
> This pure and sublime spirit
> > penetrates to the divine will
> Found at the heart of all spiritual qualities.
> It is intelligent, sacred, true to itself,
> > varied, invisible,
> Full of power, piercing, clean;
> Full of light, benevolence, direction;
> Full of love for humanity,
> Irresistible to mankind;
> A true source of stability and endurance,
> Complete in divine love, wisdom, and power.
> This spirit is the breath of the will of God.

What a tremendous description of virtue, our link to divine wisdom, love, beauty, harmony, peace, and grace! From Solomon's description, it becomes clear that virtue is the link that connects us to the active power within any divine quality, be it wisdom or anything else. It is virtue that enables us to enter into Emerson's transcendent life; lacking virtue, we are still ignorant of our true human nature and birthright.

The ministry of the Christ also demonstrates the vital necessity of virtue. One of the most dramatic moments in the New Testament is when Jesus asks John to baptize him. John demurs, protesting, "It is I who need baptizing by you, and yet you come to me!" Jesus then answers: "It is proper to baptize me at this time; virtue demands it."

Once the baptism was completed, God descended upon Jesus in the form of a dove and pronounced, "This is my beloved Son, in whom I am well pleased."

Although the moral excellence of virtue was already completely developed within Jesus, the ritual of baptism was needed to make apparent to the world the inner aureole of virtue which connected the Christ with God. It enabled God to put an "extra charge" into Jesus's expression of divine perfection. Even though our expression of virtue is not likely to be so complete or powerful, it is important to comprehend that virtue is a part of our spiritual life. We must strive to express it as a constant factor in our life.

It is interesting to note that Jesus was not baptised

in order to be saved, or even as a sign that he had been reborn. He was baptised in order to fulfill the demand of virtue—a virtue that had already been brought to a level of perfection within him. In the Christian church, therefore, it would make more sense to view baptism as a sign that a commitment has been made to spirit, rather than as a badge of redemption.

Jesus, of course, did express virtue as a constant part of his ministry. He did not just preach and cajole; he healed and performed miracles. Each one was a demonstration of the power of virtue.

Perhaps the most remarkable in this regard was the healing of the woman who had hemorrhaged for twelve years. She had been to all of the medical experts, but they could do nothing to help her. One day, as Jesus was hurrying to the home of a person who was ill, the woman approached his entourage. She could only get near enough to touch the hem of his garment, but felt that even this slight contact would be enough to heal her distress. In an instant, she felt the virtue of the Christ enter her own body and stop the bleeding. But in the same instant, Jesus felt the drain upon his virtue, and stopped to inquire: "Who has touched my robe?" Frightened and trembling, the woman came forward and told him her story. In his turn, the Christ blessed her, saying: "Courage, my daughter; your faith has restored you to health. Go in peace and be freed of your discomfort."

This story drives home the immense power within virtue. It is the power within human wisdom, the power within human benevolence. But it is also the power within healing and all apparent miracles. No one is without virtue; it is part of our heritage. But most people have little skill in using the virtue within them, either to regain access to Paradise or to enrich the power of their self-expression.

A Source of Strength

Virtue is not just an antiquarian oddity that has no relevance to our modern lives. It is just as much our birthright—our key to the gates of Eden—today as it was two or three thousand years ago. In point of fact, since most major religions have lost sight of the esoteric meaning of virtue, our need to cultivate virtue has become far more urgent than ever.

It does not matter what our attitudes and beliefs about God are, nor which religious creeds or rituals we obey. Virtue is important to every one of us, whether we be Hindu, Christian, Jew, Moslem, Buddhist, or even atheist. Every one of us has lungs, without regard to whether the vitality we breathe is prana or pneuma or just the breath of life. Just so, every one of us has virtue, regardless of the brand of dogma we choose to use to cope with our personal confusion. If we ignore the presence of virtue within us and fail to cultivate it, we handicap ourself greatly, just as a person with two good lungs handicaps himself immensely by smoking. Ignoring the virtue within us does not necessarily make us evil, nor does it condemn us to an eternity in hell. It does not make us less of a human being. It just compounds our ignorance and suffering.

Indeed, we can be a fundamentalist or a permissionary, a liberal or a conservative. We can be of any racial or ethnic background. The labels matter not. We all need virtue—and we need it today as much as Solomon needed it three thousand years ago.

Why is this so? There are two points we need to understand:

First, God does not abandon His creation. He is just as much present in our lives encouraging us to discover the virtue within us today as He ever has been. As a society, we may be ignoring God more than ever before, debating whether or not He is dead, but God is not ignoring us. He is still vitally involved in our lives, our growth, and our culture. We therefore need virtue now more than ever.

Second, society is undergoing tremendous changes which are every bit as rough and tumultuous as the waters Jesus had to calm when the boat in which his disciples were sailing threatened to capsize. In a very short period of time, we have moved from an agrarian society to an industrial society to an electronic society. The old systems of caste and class have been discarded. Women are demanding their just share. Old habits and traditions are being challenged and discarded at an unprecedented rate. Hardly anyone has been immune to the impact of this rapid change.

Virtue is an indispensable source of strength and stability during such times of change. It is to our discredit that we have spurned virtue at the very moment we most need it, but even this is understandable. Confronted with these vast changes, some of the thinking members of the race have looked at traditional meanings of virtue—the simple definition of virtue as goodness and morality—and realized that a strict moral code has often done more to create modern conflicts than to show us how to resolve them. The Catholic Church's strong stand against birth control in any form, in the name of morality, has created a conflict that defies common sense. In so doing, it is serving unthinking tradition far more than it is serving virtue—or morality.

In such an environment of religious hypocrisy, it is not surprising that skeptics are prone to disregard virtue altogether. But the impact of discarding virtue is devastating, both on the individual and on society. It is virtue that links us to the absolutes of life, be they the Absolutes of Plato, the Absolutes of Lao Tsu, or the Absolutes of Solomon. It is virtue that gives us the strength to endure great change with humor and grace. It is virtue that enables us to withstand sharp personal pain and even humiliation and continue to strive to serve our design for this life as best we can.

With these two basic principles in mind, it is then possible to survey the many benefits that a strong life of virtue brings us, both individually and collectively:

Virtue connects us with our divine design. To whatever degree we have learned to honor and express divine ideals such as joy, harmony, beauty, and peace, we have learned to respond to a basic wavelength of divine life. We have been touched by a fragment of spirit, and it is forever a part of our being and consciousness. Through this contact, which is the beginning seed of virtue, we learn to respond to the divine design of our soul for us. This blueprint may inspire us to develop artistic talents, to lead others, or to teach or to serve; the specific activity does not matter. What counts is the fact that we are responding to a true contact with spirit. Virtue is growing within us.

Virtue impels us toward excellence in all that we do. Life presents us with tasks to perform. Our task may be as simple as digging ditches, or as complex as helping mankind travel in outer space. A task may be shared with millions of others, or it may be ours alone. But whatever the task may be, we are called to perform it with the very best attention and talents that we have—the highest level of excellence that we can reach. Every task gives us an opportunity to treat other people with respect, to handle authority wisely, to grasp the larger picture or purpose, and to take pride in the contribution we are making to the welfare of humanity. Just being self-reliant is a great blessing on society!

Virtue inspires a healthy self-esteem, reminding us that we are always connected to God. Many people in our modern society suffer unnecessarily from emotional imbalances. They have separated themselves from the virtue within themselves, within humanity, and within society, and have turned instead to violence, drugs, and hedonism to try to fill the void. But the void just becomes greater. The cultivation of virtue, on the other hand, reminds us that part of our inner being is dynamically connected to God, no matter how distorted and corrupted our physical life may be. We are a child of God, cut from cosmic fabric. Our life counts.

Virtue compels us to choose the most ethical option whenever confronted by difficult decisions. The principle of duality (as expressed by the yang and the yin of Chinese philosophy) guarantees that our life will be filled with difficult decisions to make. In the process, we have the chance to increase our wisdom. But far too many people try to choose between the two best possibilities as presented by physical circumstances. They fail to look within themselves, and harness the capacity of virtue to help them see the larger picture involved. If we have been betrayed by a friend, for example, the choice seems to be between a) pretending that the betrayal never happened, thus preserving a friendship; and b) taking action to let the friend know that we know—and stoutly disapprove. But both of these common options overlook the third option, the option of virtue. Understanding our friend's self-centeredness, we forgive him for his betrayal and get on with the business of living. We take this episode in stride, understanding that we too have occasionally let down our friends, and that the offense does not merit a hysterical reaction. In this fashion, we harness the virtue of goodwill and direct it into our character and lifestyle.

Virtue fortifies us with infinite strength to cope with disasters. Unpleasant events occasionally happen in physical life. We get fired. Friends die. We suffer financial losses. We are disappointed. These circumstances can shock and dismay us, sending us into a downward spiral of depression. But this kind of reaction is never necessary. We become depressed when we try to cope with the discouraging aspects of life with materialistic skills and options only. Virtue, by contrast, keeps us continually linked with the very essence of divine life. It renews us daily with the fortitude and courage we need to meet crisis and disaster head on, with the best within us. This strength of virtue is more than just a blind trust in God. It is an actual perception that part of our inner life has been saturated with divine power, and that this power can be summoned by us at any time to triumph over pain and opposition.

Virtue stimulates growth. Each of us is on a journey of self-discovery. We can pursue this trek in blindness, or we can pursue it with the wisdom of virtue. We can rebel against our inner nature, or we can invite it to help us negotiate the traps and land mines that may be awaiting us. The more we recognize the benevolent presence of spirit in our life, through the medium of virtue, the more we can enjoy the growth we are making.

Virtue refreshes and heals us. We all suffer from fatigue. But it is only the force of materialism that wears us down. The inner presence of virtue acts upon us in exactly the opposite way. It opens our eyes to new opportunities. It heals us when we become infirm. It reminds us that the power of God is, indeed, the power to make all things new.

Even our attitudes about the role that virtue should play in our lives can be reviewed, revised, and updated!

Stealing from Angels

As important as virtue obviously is to our sanity and stability, most of us nonetheless do more to ignore virtue than to cultivate it. In part, this shunning of virtue has been encouraged by the impoverished intellectual climate of our times. But most of the blame lies with the traditional ways in which we cope with the surprises of life.

There are three primary ways we wall ourselves off from the active presence of virtue in our lives. These three are:

We become absorbed in our personal problems and wallow in self-pity. Solomon stated it clearly: "The selfish divorce themselves from God." In our society, the tendency of special interest groups to place their programs ahead of the common weal is a blatant sign of our modern lack of virtue. This selfishness has torn apart the fabric of our civilization, leading to unrestrained litigation in our courts, unbalanced programs to protect very narrow interests, and a widespread malaise among the voting populace. In the individual, the current obsession with being a "victim" also exposes the modern decline into selfishness. A victim is nothing more than a person without the virtue to overcome his or her own hardships, whatever they may be.

**We become bitter, because we think that life has

treated us unfairly. Bitter people resent every bump they have had to endure along the road of life, and carry this baggage of bitterness with them wherever the road takes them. These people need to learn the lesson Krishna taught Arjuna in the *Bhagavad-Gita:*

>In the beginning, God created all men
>And assigned each a duty.
>"Do this, and you shall prosper," he said.
>"Duty performed with excellence
>Honors the angels and leads to virtue.
>In their turn, the angels will lift up
>Men and women of virtue:
>In this way, men and women reach the Highest.
>Please the angels
>   and your requests shall be granted.
>But the person who enjoys the bounty of life
>And shows no gratitude
>Steals from the angels."

A bitter, resentful person is enslaved by the circumstances that embittered him. These memories divorce him from God and make him incapable of gratitude. As a result, he ends up "stealing from angels." He is a person without virtue.

Jealousy and hate work in exactly the same way. **We plunge ourselves into materialism.** As Jesus told us at the Sermon on the Mount, human beings cannot serve both God and mammon. Mammon is the spirit of desire; it is a poor substitute for virtue. In short, the Christ was telling us that we make choices every day which will either strengthen or deplete our virtue. To the degree that we act as though our life ends with the death of the physical form, we are immersed in materialism. To the degree that we act as though only the inner virtues of spirit matter, we have liberated ourselves from materialism. This is not just a simple matter of greed, however. We plunge ourselves into materialism whenever we become discouraged, depressed, or disappointed in life. The reward of a virtuous life is the ability to enjoy the grand drama of evolution and the glorious wonders of Creation, even while laboring to help others escape the pitfalls and imperfections of materialism.

The price we pay for indulging in self-pity, bitterness, or materialism is beyond calculation. No, we are not condemned to rot forever in hell. But who needs hell as a vehicle for punishment, when the state of being estranged from the very best and purest within us is the obvious consequence of pursuing a life without virtue? Without virtue, there is no divine protection to preserve our physical health. Without virtue, we brand ourselves with a stigma to which other humans react unconsciously. Without virtue, we become desolate, lonely, and alienated. Without virtue, we become confused, unable to discern the way ahead of us. Without virtue, we become like Esau. We have sold our birthright and our blessing.

It is not surprising that "alienation" has become a major theme in the twentieth century, shaping human thought from Marxism to Existentialism and beyond. Alienation is at the heart of the great divisions of human society—for example, the supposed division between the "haves" and the "have nots."

Alienation is a bogus belief. For alienation to have any credibility as a theory, it must exclude any sense of virtue and embrace pure materialism. Even then, the worst damage it can do is to cause good people to forget their divine birthright, and try to live life without virtue.

Of course, it cannot be done. Virtue is a dynamic part of our lives, individually and collectively, and we cannot long deny it. We can pretend that it does not exist, but eventually our pretense will be shattered. We are designed to act with virtue. We can torture ourselves by refusing to embrace virtue, but we cannot kill it. Sooner or later, virtue will call to us—and we shall respond.

It should be clear even to materialists that the ancient axiom, "the sooner the better," still applies.

Let us love virtue.

Split in Halves

How did virtue come to be so demeaned in our thinking? It is a natural process, actually. In order to be responsive to our inner virtue, we must be open to its presence. If we come to believe that virtue is nothing more than a moral code of ethics, it will not occur to us to seek out our inner treasure of virtue and tap it. We are far more likely to leap to the conclusion that because we have thought through the serious ethical issues of human life, we are a person of virtue.

Herein lie the seeds of mischief. Virtue is not an intellectual concept, to be debated as if it were no more significant than the outcome of a political contest. Virtue is our growing responsiveness to the will of God, as it applies both to humanity as a whole and to each of us individually. As this virtue pervades our consciousness, it does indeed begin to govern our ethics and our behavior. But good, decent behavior is a consequence of virtue, not a cause of it.

Socrates, Xenophon, and Plato knew this about virtue; so did Solomon, Krishna, and Lao Tsu. The Christ demonstrated it repeatedly. But all too often, the "thinkers" of human society fail to grasp the truth that has already been laid out for all to see and be guided by. Having never experienced virtue in their lives, some of these thinkers have cheapened it into a mere intellectual premise. Others began debating it. Those in turn were eventually followed by lesser thinkers who debunked it. This is the way ignorance spreads throughout society.

Actually, one group responsible for cheapening virtue is also one that deserves huge credit for promoting it—the Roman Catholic Church. Once St. Augustine had codified the seven cardinal virtues, the machinery of the church turned the vital presence of virtue into the dead stone of dogma. As a result, virtue ceased being a dynamic interaction with the divine design of life and became only a set of rules for ethical behavior. The practice of virtue was thought to include such aberrations as mortification of the flesh, poverty of spirit, and chastity.

There is certainly nothing wrong with anyone being guided by a coherent set of ethical principles. Ideally, however, these principles emerge out of the individual's intelligent interaction with virtue, rather than a subservient obeisance to dogma. By removing the presence of divine life from virtue, Catholic theologians carelessly misled millions of people throughout the centuries.

For a thousand years, the reality of virtue lay buried, encrusted in a tomb of theology. But virtue cannot be suppressed, even unintentionally.

During this period of time—the Dark Ages and the Middle Ages—virtue remained a dominant theme within the church. But the importance of virtue was kept primarily within the cloistered walls of the church's orders. It did not play a major role in the secular world, save in works of art. The portrayal of the key virtues was one of the favorite themes of art throughout Europe.

Gradually, the intense focus on virtue within the church began to seep into secular culture and awareness. Dante Alighieri, writing in the early fourteenth century, stated that "everything is virtuous in its nature when it does what it is ordained to do." Two centuries later, Niccólo Machiavelli also became absorbed in the discussion of virtue. In *The Prince*, he states that a conventional sense of moral goodness (as defined by society) might actually prevent a man of virtue from acting in accord with his spiritual design, especially if he is a leader or general. In this regard, Machiavelli, who is frequently attacked for his "might makes right" approach to life, echoes Krishna's counsel to Arjuna. Machiavelli referred to men of virtue as *virtuosi,* a label that is still used to refer to people of great talent and inspiration. He did not limit *virtuosi* to the field of music, however; he regarded great leaders, mystics, and scientific geniuses as people of virtue.

While Machiavelli had a number of important

insights into the nature of virtue, ultimately he ended up distorting virtue as much as describing it. He missed the point that virtue links humanity with God; therefore, the spiritual ideals of divine life pervade the entire life and ethics of the *virtuosi*. The virtuous person cannot help expressing virtue; it would be a denial of his very character to do so.

The full rebirth of virtue within the world at large came during the Renaissance. A book by St. Francis de Sales, *Introduction to the Devout Life*, became wildly popular throughout Europe when it was first published in 1609. Books were still a rare commodity at this time, and a starving reading public hungrily devoured it. His description of virtue set the tone for intellectual and religious discussion of the topic for hundreds of years.

Much of the *Introduction to the Devout Life* is beautifully written and helpful even today. St. Francis is quite modern in his comments on eliminating anxiety and fear from our lives, and advocating patience. But he extols the practice of self-abasement to the point where it could do psychogical harm if anyone implemented his suggestions.

Having set the tone, the discussion of virtue quickly grew. In Italy, the cradle of the Renaissance, two distinct meanings of virtue emerged:

Virtú, which defined the moral perfection of the human character.

Virtù, which decribed the inner essence of power in any person or thing.

The wholeness of virtue had thus been split in half, with each half conveying only part of the truth. Put together, the two definitions do a fairly good job at conveying the importance of virtue. Kept separate, however, both fail to embrace the reality. Worse, the two definitions encouraged "thinkers" to take sides and debate the one against the other. Which is exactly what they did.

As a popular idea, virtue rose to great heights during this time. In an age when fortune held sway over the thinking of most people, virtue was viewed as a force of equal importance. Man could not sway fortune, but he could choose to act with virtue. Virtue was therefore the key to human freedom, liberation, and transcendence.

In England, the examination of virtue saturates the pages of the more serious poems of the satirist Alexander Pope, *The Essay on Man* and *The Moral Essays.* Indeed, virtue is the "hero" of *The Essay on Man,* the culmination of a lengthy exploration of the nature of man and our relationship with God. In Pope's cosmology, virtue still derives from the divine design:

> Ere Wit oblique had broke that steady light,
> Man, like his Maker, saw that all was right.

> To Virtue, in the Paths of Pleasure, trod,
> And owned a Father when he owned a God.

In fact, Pope makes it abundantly clear that virtue links us to the divine life, and cannot be understood in materialistic terms alone:

> What nothing earthly gives, or can destroy,
> The soul's calm sunshine, and the heartfelt joy,
> Is Virtue's prize: A better would you fix?
> Then give Humility a coach and six,
> Justice a Conqueror's sword, or Truth a gown,
> Or Public Spirit its great cure, a Crown.

The dominance of virtue as a keystone in human thinking lasted through the Enlightenment, the age in which scientific thinking grew at an accelerated rate. The Age of Enlightenment was followed, however, by the Age of Revolution—a time when traditional systems and values were discarded throughout the world in favor of new ideas—democracy, individuality, and freedom. The idea of virtue, which had ruled the world of human thought for three centuries, was an obvious target.

Rousseau led the charge, arguing that virtue derived from the natural order of physical life. Others opined that the only true virtue was self-preservation. This set the stage for the theories of alienation of Marx, and virtue became completely disconnected from divine life and will. The intellectual destruction of virtue became complete with the advent of existentialism, which hypothesized that the circumstances we experience throughout life are the primary determinant of our ethics and principles.

The result has been the unwelcomed appearance of relativism. Relativism is a direct assault on virtue, because it rejects the importance of a divine design for life, founded on absolute principles. In relativism, truth is always in the eye of the beholder. Anything goes. Thus, on the day of the only impeachment of an elected President in America's history, the vice-president stated that he thought the President would be remembered in history as one of the nation's greatest. Such a conclusion betrays the rampant influence of relativism. The vice-president was saying, in effect, "The vote of impeachment is just your opinion. Here's mine." It skirted the whole issue of dishonesty, criminal misconduct, and other travesties of virtue.

It is hard to imagine Socrates responding in this way. In fact, he did not. When sentenced to death on trumped-up charges, he accepted the decision. His captors left open the door to his cell in the hope that he would escape into exile and save Athens a tremendous embarrassment, but he did not. Socrates drank the hemlock. In so doing, he was guided by virtue. Not self-preservation. Not relativism (well, everyone is doing it, so why shouldn't I). Not even moral goodness (his students all wanted him to save himself). As recorded by Plato, Socrates explained his decision in this way:

"Because I have been happy to live in Athens for thirty years and have benefited from its laws, it would be wrong for me now to decide that those laws no longer apply to me." Socrates truly knew the power of virtue, and lived his life accordingly.

But it is not just the Presidency that has been poisoned by relativism. When teachers complain to parents about the unruly and rude behavior of their children, the parents frequently defend their children and assail the teachers—sometimes violently. Such behavior would never happen in a society of virtue. It can only happen when sentimental feelings toward the child are given more importance than the child's need to grow up and learn adult behavior.

The loss of virtue in our society has been a tragic one. It colors every facet of our thinking and search for meaning. One of the primary ideals of American life, for example, is freedom. But freedom is an elusive state. It is much, much more than just the absence of tyranny. Freedom requires its citizens to cooperate with each other intelligently and responsibly. It guarantees individual rights, to be sure, but only to the degree that those rights are exercised with responsibility.

As long as virtue was viewed as an asset in America, the innate conflict between rights and responsibility did not become a major issue. But during this last century, the loss of virtue has been catastrophic. As a result, there is more and more discussion of "rights" that are not and never have been rights, and less and less examination of "responsibility."

It is not the fault of the "thinkers" of society that virtue has fallen from conventional grace, however. We each have a duty to think for ourself. It may be true that Plato postulated everything we need to know about virtue; it may be equally true that Diderot, Rousseau, and Sartre were confused thinkers guilty of "mind crimes" against humanity. So what? Each of us has a mind of our own. We are meant to use it to think through the vital issues of life and make up our own minds about them—not just take the word of some long-dead philosopher, theologian, or expert.

Academic philosophy is teetering on the brink of irrelevancy; it would be a blessing if religious theology came to the same fate. But this is not to suggest that philosophy and theology have no meaning to us. It is simply time for each of us to discover the value of practical philosophy and practical theology in our lives.

The subject of virtue is a great place to start. Each of us must decide:

Will I be a Prohibitionary, demanding that the government establish and enforce a strict moral code of behavior?

Will I be a Permissionary, demanding that the government protect my right to do anything I want, as long as it does not seem to harm anyone?

Or will I be a lover of virtue, tolerating both the Prohibitionaries and the Permissionaries, but laboring to restore virtue to its proper pre-eminence in human thinking?

Vice—Or Virtue?

In the effort to understand virtue, many people make the mistake of concluding that it is merely the absence of vice. In fact, once the Catholic church had enshrined the seven cardinal virtues, it felt obliged to produce a list of seven deadly sins. But the cultivation of virtue is not a war against vice. It is a steady progression toward God.

In discussing the vastly different natures of vice and virtue in Book II of *The Essay on Man,* Pope reminds us that virtue can be studied only as a complete whole:

> Let subtle schoolmen teach these friends to fight,
> More studious to divide than to unite;
> And Grace and Virtue, Sense and Reason split,
> With all the rash dexterity of wit.
> Wits, just like Fools, at war about a name,
> Have full as oft no meaning, or the same.

The absence of vice is a state of naïveté similar to the "innocence" of Adam and Eve in the garden of Eden. It is an innocence based entirely on ignorance and lack of experience. Until Eve eats symbolically of knowledge, she is unaware of vice and temptation. In such a state, it is "natural" to be innocent and good.

Virtue, by contrast, is the inner maturity which comes to us as we choose to sublimate our human desires and focus our awareness more and more at the level of divine life. Having tasted of cruelty, we decide it makes far more sense to be guided by goodwill. Having inflicted and endured harm, we decide that it is far better to be inspired by helpfulness. Having been thwarted by laziness, we decide that the best option is to take initiative in our life.

Vices can be controlled by social laws and conventions; every dictatorship has proven it. But virtue cannot be legislated. It depends entirely upon the willingness of the individual to recognize his or her divine birthright and respond to it. We can encourage others to aspire to virtue, but there is absolutely no way any one of us can force anyone else to become virtuous.

When moral goodness is the sole object of virtue, the practice of virtue quickly disintegrates into the avoidance of vice. Instead of focusing our attention on cultivating helpfulness, patience, and harmony, we preoccupy ourself with the much more strenuous work of avoiding "sin." We are also apt to objectify vices in the form of physical habits—the vices of smoking, drinking, drug usage, gambling, and sex. This is a red herring. It is true that when indulged to excess, any of these practices can become addictions—traps which may cause us to forget our divine nature. But many people of great virtue have smoked heavily, drunk a bit too much, and enjoyed sex, without any of these habits diminishing their virtue.

Few physical vices keep people from cultivating virtue. The real problems are far more likely to be emotionally or mentally based. One of the greatest of all vices, from this perspective, is passiveness. A second is hypocrisy. Others would include anxiety, fear, doubt, insecurity, and impatience.

For this reason, there is no compelling reason why government should ever try to legislate moral goodness. We should remember the advice of Thomas Paine, and rely on the virtue of our fellow citizens. Less harm can come from an occasional adult watching a pornographic movie than from government at any level trying to legislate vice out of existence. The inability to eliminate vice forcibly was clearly demonstrated by the fiasco of the Holy Inquisition. Intended to force people to act morally, it quickly became a breeding ground for the worst kind of evil. More recently, Prohibition met the same fate, leading not to the eradication of drinking but rather to the rise and establishment of organized crime in America.

This is not to say, however, that government should actually promote pornography (or any other vice)—for example, by giving subsidies to movie theaters that disseminate it. This would be silly. But government compounds the problem by trying to defeat it—and at the same time causes government to become larger. In a society that valued adult responsibility, pornography could never flourish. There would therefore be no need for government intervention.

Indeed, if movie producers in general were expected to be people of virtue—*virtuosi* in its true sense—they would cease producing movies that pander to the baser human instincts. Films that are designed to induce horror and shock are far more obscene, from the standpoint of virtue, than many of the films showing in X-rated theaters. Films that encourage youth to shoot up their schools are likewise an affront to virtue. But they should not be banned by law. They must be banned instead by public action—by cultivating a stronger awareness of virtue, so that the public is no longer responsive to such portrayals.

If we truly love virtue, vice has no appeal. It disappears entirely off the radar screen of our perception. We are inspired instead by the active, vital presence of virtue deep within us.

Taking Charge

The work of cultivating virtue occurs in two dimensions simultaneously. First, we must clean up our mental and emotional households eliminating any tendencies toward unethical behavior. At the same time, we must open our mind and become responsive to the divine spirit within us. Virtue, after all, is our capacity to identify with our inner design for perfection and excellence, and then express it in meaningful ways as we interact with life. Without responsiveness to spirit, virtue is reduced to a trivial, intellectual concept. But by the same token, without a heartfelt effort to clean up our ethical household, the soul will not respond, no matter how hard we pray, meditate, or invoke.

The most important ingredient in this work is taking charge of our own thinking. We must review every ethical principle that we hold and cherish, and ask ourself: "From what source did I derive this belief? Did I learn it at home, in church, at school, or from society?" Once we have identified the source, we must next evaluate its veracity. Did the minister who taught me this principle understand it himself? Or was he just spouting dogma?

An excellent question to ask at this stage of our review is: "Has this principle helped me or harmed me since I adopted it?" Has it added greater stability to our values and ethics, or has it led instead to one crisis of conscience after another? Has it helped us understand life, or just confused us?

This review may lead to extensive investigation of the underlying ideas that gave birth to this principle. In considering the ethical weight of original sin in our thinking, for example, it may be helpful to know that the doctrine of original sin was invented by St. Augustine four centuries after the death of Jesus. The Christ never mentioned or alluded to original sin. In fact, Augustine developed this theoretical concept in refutation of the beliefs of a Christian monk in England, Pelagius, who was encouraging his flock to think for themselves and discover the inner realities of God through their individual meditations.

Pelagius taught the very modern view that God only wants us to live good, virtuous lives—but if we are bad, it is our own shortcoming. To Augustine, this teaching smacked of heresy; it gave human beings far too much power over their destiny, thereby making God look weak. So out of the necessity to stop Pelagius, Augustine developed the doctrine of predestination. This doctrine held that God, being Omniscient, knows what all our decisions will be long before we make them. Indeed, He knew, as early as the dawn of Creation, that Judas would betray Jesus—according to Augustine.

The doctrine of predestination had just one major flaw (other than being false); it led to the question: "Why bother with Creation if every act and thought is predestined? Is it just a giant game of divine Solitaire?" Augustine answered with another all-new doctrine: original sin. This theory teaches that we are all stained by the fall of Adam and Eve; the purpose of Creation is to test us. If we believe in God, we will be saved. If not, we will be doomed forever to hell.

Original sin, therefore, has no basis in any teaching of the Christ. It was invented by St. Augustine for the purpose of discrediting Pelagius and forestalling Christians from embracing a principle of spiritual accountability. Not even the fact that the doctrine of original sin has been passed from priest to priest over the centuries and taught to billions of believing Christians can make it truthful or helpful to the virtuous life.

By reviewing each of our principles and beliefs in this fashion, we slowly establish a baseline of values about how we want to act in life. We must then develop techniques for actually disciplining the emotions and our desires so that we act consistently with these principles. Whenever we find ourself straying from our established baseline, we must gently and patiently refocus our thoughts and actions so that they become consistent once again.

It is likewise important to study the spiritual ideals or qualities on which we want to base this foundation of ethical behavior. The divine energy of joy is not at all like the common human expressions of happiness or pleasure. To be inspired by the virtue of joy, therefore, we must read about joy, try to contact it in our personal reflections, and open our mind and heart to the inflow of the genuine divine article—not just our own variation on the theme. This investigation requires a bit of work; it is not as simple as logging onto the Internet and expecting *Yahoo!* to pinpoint an accurate definition of joy if we enter the word in its search function. We must develop a set of reliable sources, and then check with them as necessary. Some of the best sources are:

• The actual words spoken by the Christ, as recorded in the Bible. Passages from other major religious scriptures may also be helpful. Theological concepts should be given no weight at all, regardless of their religious origin.

• The writings of inspired thinkers such as Plato, Lao Tsu, Ralph Waldo Emerson, René Descartes, Alexander Pope, and others.

• The essays of *The Art of Living* and *The Life of Spirit* series, many of which are commentaries on a specific virtue: Joy, Courage, Peace, Patience, Goodwill, Beauty, Integrity, and many more. Of special value is the essay, "Becoming Graceful," which presents a highly effective meditative tool for becoming more spiritually graceful in our self-expression.

- The I Ching. This is an ancient Chinese text heavily steeped in the development of a virtuous lifestyle. It is a system of practical philosophy which can help anyone to develop a coherent set of values and principles, thereby providing a strong foundation for cultivating virtue.

By reading about the virtues in this way, we stock our mental household with inspiring thoughts and ideas. But the mere absorption of these ideas does not guarantee that we will acquire virtue. In addition to reading about spiritual qualities, we must think about them. We must imagine acting with divine strength or harmony or courage. We should try to visualize calling on these inner reserves when tempted to act in selfish ways. In this way, we register the inner force of these qualities in our own structure of character, deep in our subconscious mind.

The need to cultivate virtue in these ways is not a new idea. In his *Autobiography*, Benjamin Franklin describes a project that he set for himself in order to cultivate a virtuous character. After much reflection, he listed thirteen qualities that he considered the virtues of human life:

"1. Temperance. Eat not to dullness. Drink not to elevation.

"2. Silence. Speak not but what may benefit others or yourself. Avoid trifling conversation.

"3. Order. Let all your things have their places. Let each part of your business have its time.

"4. Resolution. Resolve to perform what you ought. Perform without fail what you resolve.

"5. Frugality. Make no expense but to do good to others or yourself; i.e., waste nothing.

"6. Industry. Lose no time. Be always employed in something useful. Cut off all unnecessary actions.

"7. Sincerity. Use no hurtful deceit. Think innocently and justly; and, if you speak, speak accordingly.

"8. Justice. Wrong none by doing injuries or omitting the benefits that are your duty.

"9. Moderation. Avoid extremes. Forbear resenting injuries so much as you think they deserve.

"10. Cleanliness. Tolerate no uncleanliness in body, clothes, or habitation.

"11. Tranquillity. Be not disturbed at trifles or at accidents common or unavoidable.

"12. Chastity. Rarely use venery but for health or offspring—never to dullness, weakness, or the injury of your own or another's peace or reputation.

"13. Humility. Imitate Jesus and Socrates."

Having compiled his list, Franklin then decided to give a week's "strict attention" to each virtue, in order, compiling his results in a notebook. This method helped him remain vigilant to live up to his goals, and quickly shaped his character as he willed it.

Franklin goes on to write that at one time he had intended to publish a book on the topic, *The Art of Virtue*, which would have shown the method and means of attaining each of these goals. It is clear that Franklin fully comprehended the meaning and value of virtue in our lives, both individually and collectively. In a note that he appended to the text of his autobiography, he wrote: "Nothing so likely to make a man's fortune as virtue."

Franklin's life and achievements demonstrate that it is both practical and useful to cultivate virtue. But it takes effort—an effort that each of us must be willing to engage in, if we love virtue.

Twelve Key Virtues

There is nothing incomplete about Plato's listing of four virtues, nor the expanded list of Plotinus, who appended the three virtues of faith, hope, and love, as enunciated by St. Paul. It would be far better for a person to start with the cultivation of just one virtue, whatever it might be, and achieve success, than to embark on an ambitious program of cultivating twenty-two virtues, and be overwhelmed. The practice of any virtue which successfully links us with the spiritual presence within us will so transform our life that we can scarcely imagine what this change will be.

As humanity grows, however, its capacity and ability to express diverse spiritual qualities expands as well. It is therefore timely to expand upon the original four and the cardinal seven. Although Franklin enumerated thirteen, he confessed that he only added humility after being prodded by a Quaker friend of his—and that he found the practice of it very taxing! Nonetheless, it should be noted that he did an admirable job of imitating at least Socrates.

For this treatise, I have chosen to focus on twelve primary spiritual attitudes which, when cultivated properly, will gradually build our individual responsiveness to the inner presence of virtue. This virtue will then pour into our life and character like a divine elixir, sweetening our disposition and maturing our behavior. It will link us with the spiritual will to discipline our thoughts and feelings, and guide our actions accordingly.

The twelve virtues we will examine for the purpose of becoming a *virtuosi* ourself are:
1. Goodwill.
2. Wisdom.
3. Generosity.
4. Courage.
5. Cheerfulness.
6. Reverence.
7. Harmony.
8. Justness.
9. Temperance.
10. Integrity.
11. Beauty.
12. Patience.

Each of these virtues will be examined in a chapter of its own. The goal in doing so is not to impose a specific interpretation of these qualities, but rather to demonstrate just how they bring the mystical force of virtue into human life.

Goodwill

The words "love," "compassion," and "goodwill" are cheapened and trivialized by unthinking people every day. Politicians who are so unprincipled that they peddle their influence for campaign contributions claim to be experts on compassion. But is their compassion real? Is it a capacity to identify with the latent impulse to grow in the recesses of a person's consciousness—or just a buzzword batted around to impress gullible voters? The tell-tale sign lies in the kinds of solutions they offer. When "compassion" is intoned in order to justify a larger government with more power over everyone's lives, it is an artifice, not the real thing. It is the painted hussy of compassion, not the living essence of it.

True compassion is the quality demonstrated by the Christ when he defended a prostitute who was about to be stoned to death. While hardly approving of her immorality, he nonetheless identified with the spark of her inner humanity. As was always the case, he understood her weakness without condemning it. Out of compassion, therefore, he called to question the motives of those who would punish her. "Let he who is without sin cast the first stone." No one could do so.

Goodwill cuts across all of the barriers that traditionally separate us. It inspires us to reach out to those who are dispossessed by war and help them rebuild their homes and cities. Compassion enables us to offer mature help wherever it is needed. It motivates the Samaritan to help the beaten Jew. Love is a divine quality that nurtures the best within us and helps us grow, both as human beings and as children of God. It is the nurturing force of a benevolent parent who always seeks what is best for his or her child.

As a virtue, goodwill inspires us to seek out, identify with, and support the growing element within any person or situation. At international levels, it enables us to see the worth of every human being on earth—and every nation. It breaks down nationalism and tribalism and promotes a climate of genuine cooperation. In the individual, the virtue of goodwill transforms our attitudes and goals so that we begin to embrace a larger and larger sphere of companionship. Instead of reserving love just for family, the virtue of goodwill helps us dismantle artificial walls of separativeness and prejudice.

Confucius considered goodwill the most important virtue of all. An ancient Chinese text on Confucianism states: "Goodwill means to love men joyously and from the innermost of one's heart." Without goodwill, Confucius taught, there can be no virtue. We become spiritually paralyzed.

The virtue of goodwill leads to the gradual development in our character of a strong sense of responsibility, a kinship with all life, and a strong love of God. As it floods into our character, it inspires us to love all that God loves and nurture all that God nurtures. It therefore reveals to us a whole new way of interacting with the rest of life. Goodwill likewise awakens us to a much larger vision of the role that humanity plays here on earth—and what it means to serve God.

As we integrate the virtue of love into our character, we will be transformed in a number of important ways:

We will be able to forgive hurts and injuries.

We will become, as St. Paul put it, "patient, kind, and capable of bearing all things, believing all things, hoping all things, and enduring all things."

We will rejoice in all that is right.

We will replace criticism with helpful support.

We will discard bitterness and learn to celebrate the wonders of God's creation.

We will strive always to build, rather than destroy.

We will value maturity and wisdom above childishness.

Wisdom

Wisdom is a powerful example of the importance of virtue. Anyone can go to school and educate the mind to work with facts and accumulate knowledge. Such people become learned. But no one can learn to be wise by studying any curriculum in school. Wisdom is generated as the mind takes the knowledge it has gathered and compares it with the basic design for this information found at spiritual levels, then integrates the resulting conclusions into its habits, character, and behavior.

If this description of wisdom seems far fetched to anyone grounded in scholastic knowledge, it can be confirmed by reading the descriptions of wisdom given to us by Socrates and Plato. Socrates was famous for never making a decision which was not inspired by his inner *daimon* or spirit. Plato's famous allegory of the Cave is entirely consistent with this approach to wisdom as well. The people staring at the images of reflected light on the wall of the cave are the gatherers of knowledge within the human family—the opinion shapers. The only people who truly understand human life are those who have left the cave and can watch events from outside (the higher forms), where they can examine the source of light and see its impact on human thinking (the lower forms).

Knowledge can be gathered and assembled without the operation of virtue. But for this knowledge to be transmuted into wisdom, virtue is an absolute necessity. The light of the divine mind must be directed upon the knowledge that has been assembled, exposing falsehoods and revealing that which is true.

Wisdom links us with the divine mind. How important is this fact to human life? To begin with, the vast majority of the emotional illnesses which are so prevalent in society today occur only because the people affected have not cultivated the virtue of wisdom. They have allowed huge dissonances and gaps to occur in their subconscious awareness—usually by failing to confront their own inconsistencies. When a person knowingly tells a lie, for example, the memory of this falsehood lingers in the subconscious, creating huge divisions. It disrupts the natural integrative processes that maintain psychological health and balance. Eventually, it results in serious inner turmoil.

As an individual learns the value of self-examination and self-discipline, however, these internal schisms can be safely confronted and healed. This is because the effort to discipline and control our thoughts and emotions draws a strong response from the soul, saturating our awareness with virtue. As we organize this inflowing virtue into a system of ethics and values, we build stability and poise.

The virtue of wisdom leads to a quickening of all of our mental skills. It furthermore gives us the ability to turn our mind toward the divine design for anything and quickly begin to understand it. As a result, it gives us a broader, more transcendent perspective on our personal problems—and on the issues and problems confronting humanity today.

Within society, the need for wisdom is great. Modern America suffers tremendously from an acceptance of mediocrity. It is assumed by far too many people that bewilderment and confusion are natural states for humanity. This is a travesty of our human potential. We need to replace the worship and adoration of the mediocre and the banal with a true respect and admiration for wisdom, genius, and achievement. We need to embrace wisdom and reward it.

Solomon described wisdom as follows:

> Wisdom is bright, and her light never fails.
> She can easily be seen by any who love her;
> She is always found by those who look for her
> So long as they look in the mind of God.
> Watch for her before confusion takes seed
> And you shall find her. She sits at your gate.

The first step toward wisdom is discipline.
To love wisdom, you must obey
    her divine design.
If you do, then wisdom will give you authority,
And you shall reign over
    ignorance and confusion.

Solomon also states: "Only through a gift from God can any human being master wisdom." This gift, of course, is virtue.

Generosity

Generosity is one of the noblest acts of human life—the act of giving time, attention, help, or money to assist someone who is struggling to improve his or her situation in life. One of the great examples of generosity is that of Andrew Carnegie, who donated most of his fortune to establishing free libraries throughout America and the world, for the purpose of making it possible for everyone to improve mentally.

Like most virtues, however, generosity has suffered somewhat by being exposed to the extreme ideas of populism and Marxism. Instead of being seen as an act of nobility, generosity has been forcibly redefined as "the transfer of wealth to the masses." Since few wealthy people volunteer to be "generous" in this way, socialists began demanding that government take over the administration of charity. The result has been serious damage to the concept of generosity—and serious damage to the masses, who have become dependent on government support.

The word "generosity" derives from the idea of "generate" or "produce." Just as a business person invests capital to generate a profit, so also the philanthropist donates his or her abundance to help improve the lot of those who still struggle. The most foolish gift is a straight handout, for it is unlikely to help the recipient improve. The best gift is usually education, because it does.

Just so, the virtue of generosity embraces a far wider range than just the act of giving money. It also includes the giving of time and skill, love and enthusiasm. The spirit of generosity drives us to nurture the best within others and within society. It inspires us to be helpful in many different ways. We can be generous with our patience, understanding, kindness, and tolerance.

Generosity is the perfect antidote to selfishness, which is one of the major barriers to virtue. Selfishness, self-centeredness, and self-pity are introverted states that isolate an individual from the rest of life. Such a person always considers his or her own interests first, and usually does not even go so far as to determine what the interests of others might be. A generous person, by contrast, has opened his mind and heart to the rest of life. He is content with what he has achieved, and now is determined to share his blessings with others. He draws life toward him, thereby enlarging the sphere of his influence.

When cultivated as a virtue, generosity links us with the divine force of Providence. Providence is the supply master of creation, the force that keeps the swallows of the air and the grain in the field nourished and healthy. It also generates opportunity. As we become truly generous in thought and feeling and deed, we are pervaded by the spiritual essence of providence. This dramatic force works at subliminal levels to help us transform our attitudes and values—to become a force of regeneration here on earth.

Thanks to the burgeoning spirit of philanthropy, generosity is a virtue that can be clearly seen at work in society. But the forces of selfishness, tribalism, and nationalism arrayed against it are formidable, and should not be discounted. It is far too easy for a business or an agency to twist generosity into an enforced exercise in selfishness—for example, by turning gift giving into a competition with other local businesses. Whenever a noble and wonderful act such as generosity becomes tainted in these ways, it becomes just a hollow ritual that has lost its soul.

Courage

Plato was quite justified in including courage among his four primary virtues, for it is one of the most difficult and sublime to attain. "Strength of heart," which is what courage literally means, is that transcendent power that emanates from the deepest recesses of our humanity. It is the ability to stand fearlessly in the light of God, no matter what abuse or opposition is thrown against us. Only a person who has obeyed the Delphic command to "know thyself" and has conquered all of his personal weaknesses can be said to express courage fully. Courage, therefore, is a hallmark of the well-integrated spiritual person.

During the Revolutionary War, General George Washington rode out from camp by himself one day, in order to be alone and reflect upon the burdens of the day. As he was returning to camp, he was confronted by a British soldier armed with a rifle. Washington was unable to reach his own gun without being shot by the soldier. Instead of making the attempt, therefore, Washington just stared at the soldier and continued riding. The soldier, frozen in his tracks by the virtue emanating from Washington, let him pass without raising his weapon.

Courage is not just defined by physical acts, however. The greatest test of courage is always our willingness to stand up for what we believe or know to be true—even in the face of opposition or threat. The person who testifies against a criminal, even though reprisals have been threatened, exhibits great courage. The nation that refuses to cave in to the demands of terrorists holding hostages demonstrates *double* courage—courage in the face of the terrorists and courage in the face of cries of protest from its own public.

Conversely, the politician who bases his votes on whether or not they will help him win re-election has no courage at all. In Thomas Paine's words, he is just a summer soldier, a sunshine patriot.

In ordinary circumstances, we are called on daily to confront with courage and mental toughness the onslaught of misinformation and lies that bombard us in the forms of advertising, the news, and social pressures. We likewise have a duty to enunciate and defend the principles and ideals we hold most dear, whenever they are being abused—or shunned.

The virtue of courage links us with divine will and divine strength. To make this connection, we must confront our fears and worries and shatter them as the illusions that they are. We must make sure that our values and principles are clear and strong—that they create an inner core of stability in our character. Having achieved this sense of poise, we must then be willing and able to identify with the power of divine life and trust in it, regardless of what might be happening to us.

The very last of the beatitudes Jesus delivered to his disciples and the gathering on the mount states: "Blessed are you when men revile you and persecute you and utter all kinds of evil against you falsely on my account. Rejoice and be glad, for your reward is great in heaven, for so men persecuted the prophets who were before you." The ability to stand steadfastly in the face of opposition creates the virtue of courage. The reward is great, for it links us with heaven—the power of God. We should therefore rejoice and be glad.

Cheerfulness

One of the most daunting problems of human civilization is the heavy pall of pessimism enveloping society. In America, this mental gloom is in part a residue of the grim sobriety of the early Puritans. But it is more than this alone. Throughout the world, as thinking people view the imperfections of human life, they become discouraged. They grow depressed. The pessimism spreads.

Such despondency estranges us even further from the heaven within us. Pessimism is a byproduct of earth alone; it does not exist in spiritual realms. Indeed, the constant mood of the soul toward life on earth is one of joy—the very same quality of joy that God expressed when He reviewed His work of creation and pronounced, "It is good."

It may seem difficult to some to sustain joy while they are dealing with the conflicts and troubles of daily life. But even these people should be able to see the value of cheerfulness as we confront the hard realities of life. A cheerful, upbeat attitude helps us stay focused on the potential behind our troubles. It helps us achieve detachment. It also enables us to transcend many problems which would otherwise drag us into the morass.

One of the biggest "downers" in modern life is the nasty belief so prevalent in America that human beings are conceived in sin, born in sin, live in sin, and die in sin; that we are lower than worms in God's estimation. How does this attitude reconcile with God's pronouncement that His creation (humanity) was good? It does not. We need a better approach. We need to learn to enjoy life and the role we play in it.

At times, it seems that laughter died years ago. Perhaps it was only made illegal, and we are all afraid to be outlaws—or at the very least, outlandish. America, after all, was a nation so strong that the Soviet Bear could not destroy it—but a nation so weak that it crumpled in the face of "political correctness." Government officials can lose their jobs for making a joke about any "serious" social issue. Men can be fired from their jobs for repeating jokes about sex they heard the night before on television. We laugh about India's sacred cows, but worship our own even more intently. We have, in the final analysis, succumbed to the dreaded disease of Namby-Pamby. We are a nation of prudes.

The rash of laughlessness has become epidemic. It cripples our inner strength and resolve. It forces us to brood upon our problems. It denies us the one outlet that can lead to transcendence.

There is only one antidote, and that is to turn back to cheerfulness, both individually and collectively. We must stop pandering to whining, childish adults who are offended by jokes and words they do not understand, and stop taking life so seriously. Life is serious, of course, but it likewise has its humorous underbelly. It is a virtue to tickle it with regularity.

The virtue of cheerfulness links us with the divine energy of joy. It steadily reminds us to pay more attention to what is right about life, rather than what is wrong. In specific, cheerfulness lets us transcend the unpleasant aspects of life (without ignoring them) and recollect the inner perfection of God's blueprint for them. It keeps us focused in the ideal, so we can confront imperfection and correct it. As such, the virtue of cheerfulness is something more than a sunny disposition. It is a trained response to hardship that lets us place the trouble we are facing within the larger context which can heal it.

Recent research confirms the value of cheerfulness. Studies have shown that people who are depressed have a much weaker immune system than people who are happy and cheerful.

Suffering is one of the most over-rated aspects of human life. It is not necessary to suffer greatly in order to grow in spirit, nor is it a virtue. Prolonged suffering traps us in our problems and primes us to start thinking like a victim. The true virtue is cheerfulness. If God views His creation with wonder and delight, so should we.

Reverence

Benjamin Franklin was correct when he left humility off his original list of virtues. Humility has too often become a "false virtue," used by certain people to keep others in subjugation. We are not designed to deny our achievements and our inner goodness. On the contrary, we are designed to transcend ordinary life and express our highest perfection. At the same time, however, it is important never to presume that we are greater than God—or greater than any other human being, for that matter. But it does not require dramatic displays of public humility to remember this fact. Self-abasement is spiritual overkill. Instead, we need *reverence*—reverence for God and all of God's life.

In many ways, reverence is the easiest and most natural of all virtues to cultivate, because God does such great work. The evidence surrounds us in all dimensions, and abounds within our own experience. Every time a handicapped child ends up teaching his or her parents the deeper meaning of patience, love, and wisdom, it is a sign to the world that God does great work. Every time a human being finds the inner strength to overcome an addiction to alcohol or drugs, it is a sign to the world that God does great things. Every time medical science discovers a new cure, or physical science discovers a new type of energy, or a poet writes a lyrical sonnet, it is a sign to the world that God performs wonders and miracles. All of these things, and so much more, should fill our minds and hearts and character with reverence.

Reverence is not just the worship of God's grandeur. It is also a celebration of all that is right and wondrous in the world. We cultivate reverence as we become aware of how perfectly the growth of life on earth fulfills its heavenly design, and how skillfully the texture of physical life is intertwined with the perfected glory of spiritual life. In return, the practice of reverence refreshes and renews our consciousness. It reveals to us the interconnectedness of all of life. With St. Francis of Assisi, we understand that we are all brothers in a single family, humanity, and likewise brothers in a larger family, God's creation. We are brothers with the animals, the plants, and even the minerals of earth. We are brothers of the angels. We should therefore respect the inner purpose and essence within each of these noble expressions of divine life.

The virtue of reverence expands our vision so that we can see how this entire scheme of life works harmoniously together. When we sing hymns to God in church or temple, our massed effort draws to us a strong angelic presence, to share in the celebration. Their presence in turn stimulates and feeds the whole of life for miles around. But it is not just in church that reverence is to be expressed. As this virtue grows, it links us to the best within life wherever we may be, whatever we may be doing.

One of the greatest indictments of the loss of virtue in our modern society is the effort to exclude prayer and religious celebration from our public schools and town halls, in the name of "religious freedom"and the separation of church and state. The misguided crusade to do this has crippled the inner development of generations of children, by divorcing them from the most natural expression of virtue. The defenders of this crusade see nothing wrong with teaching warfare, cruelty, and violence to children, but protest any practice of goodness. This stand is corrupt and devoid of wisdom.

To love virtue, we must be unafraid to love God. We must be ready to take our lamp to the top of the hill, so it may shine on all below, not hide it in a bushel basket. Only those who are so ignorant that they have never experienced the light of God could possibly have an objection to the regular practice of reverence—in schools, in government, and wherever men and women congregate.

Let us therefore confess what we know to be true: God does great things. Through the practice of the virtue of reverence, we are able to participate in this great work.

Harmony

Human beings like to create conflict. We insist on disagreeing with friends and associates, often just to explore the opposite point of view. We misconstrue helpful hints and suggestions as insults, and use the imagination to magnify minor rebuffs into capital offenses. If there is nothing else to complain about, we will be dissatisfied with the weather, the time allotted to us to complete some project, or the habits and customs of "other" people.

God does not create conflict. We do it all on our own, by being hurt, dissatisfied, or displeased. We believe that we are defending and protecting our vital interests, but in truth, we are usually just creating conflict. We always blame the other party, of course, but the act of scapegoatism does not change reality. It is still *our* conflict.

When conflict escalates, we sometimes lose self-control. In mild circumstances, we demonize and vilify our opposition. In more heated instances, our irritation may grow into anger and hatred. We may spurn the other party—or launch a vendetta. In extreme cases, conflict may lead to violence.

Society tries to control violence by restricting guns or by limiting bombs, but these steps are not genuine solutions. Ireland, Israel, and the Balkans were every bit as much the tinderboxes they are today when the only weapons available were swords. The problem is the antagonisms that have developed between the peoples involved.

Antagonisms cannot be eradicated by decree or treaty, or even by beating swords into plowshares. Animosity must be replaced by maturity and tolerance. The conflicts must be resolved at the point where they began, inside our breasts. We must reconcile ourselves with the things that upset us.

This is the work of harmony. It is cultivated by making a determined effort to respond to the best within everything in our life, rather than the worst. Discord arises whenever we view ourself as separate from others, the world, or God. It magnifies whatever we find lacking or marred, until we begin to believe that we can only be happy by removing "the problem" from our life. In this way, it generates a "problem consciousness" that poisons our ability to understand life and respond to God.

Discord is healed by recognizing that even the imperfection that annoys us has a divine element within it that is perfect. To be responsive to God, we must also be responsive to the divine perfection within this annoying part of our life. Through harmony, we learn to respond to this inner divine perfection, even as we continue to deal with its flawed expression on earth.

It is important to understand that all of the seeming conflicts in life are illusions we have created and inflicted upon ourself. The gap that exists between ourself and a competitor is just a measure of the disharmony in our own character. As we grow in our ability to define the common ground between us and the rest of life, the virtue of harmony blossoms like a spring bud within our character.

The need for the virtue of harmony in society is staggering. We have become a nation of people beset by road rage, child abuse, hatred, and stress. The schisms within society seem to be widening, like continental shelves drifting apart, rather than diminishing. Workers distrust management, and management is often out of touch with workers. Ethnic groups take pride in being different, rather than allowing the "melting pot" to transform them into Americans.

The good news is that the virtue of harmony is "user friendly." We do not have to be part of a huge association to act with harmony. As we cultivate this virtue individually, and apply it in our own life unilaterally, the magic of harmony begins to work. Other people begin to respond to our efforts, and discover that they can act with harmony as well. The influence spreads rapidly, once one person takes up the challenge.

The virtue of harmony connects us with divine harmony and divine order—powerful forces which govern our lives in ways most of us do not even suspect. A person in harmony with life is therefore a person who can act with enormous impact. He can lead and inspire. He can heal discords. He can create opportunities for successful action.

The greatest result of cultivating the virtue of harmony, however, occurs within us. In our modern day, it is not uncommon to find people who have let life ravage them psychologically. Their potential for inner peace and stability has been torn asunder by silly hatreds, bitter reactions to life, and illusory expectations. They are at war with themselves. The practice of psychiatry has helped some of these people to restore inner balance, but there is still much about the human unconscious and character that is unknown even by psychiatry. The person who strives to cultivate harmony invokes an inflow of divine harmony which helps repair any damage that has been done, generating a new level of maturity and contentment.

It is sad that any human being should be discontented with life. We are blessed with a birthright rich in potential and enjoyment. It is therefore important to discover the virtue of harmony. As we learn to respond to the inner richness of every one and every thing, the long "winter of our discontent" fades and is replaced by true fulfillment.

Few transformations are more significant.

Justness

We have an unfortunate tendency to equate "justice" with punishment. If we harm someone, we must pay a penalty, in order to learn not to commit harm. While this principle is true, it is usually misunderstood. To comprehend the virtue of justice, we must reverse our attempt to define it. Instead of emphasizing the punishment that befalls those who err, we should underscore the importance of acting always in accord with our divine design. This is the meaning of justness.

The first characteristic of a just person, therefore, is that the mind has been trained to respond to inner guidance. The just person is able to tap divine guidance and translate it into powerful and effective action.

Human history provides us with many excellent examples of just people. Socrates, who never acted unless inspired by his *daimon*, is one. Solomon is another. In more recent times, Abraham Lincoln would be an outstanding example.

The cultivation of justness as a virtue teaches us the link between cause and effect. Again, we often think of this issue negatively, in terms of punishment. But most of the causes and effects in our lives are positive and benevolent. Whenever we help another person, we set in motion causes that lead eventually to new opportunities. Whenever we adhere to our principles, we generate causes that strengthen us. Whenever we grow in maturity, we unleash causes that expand the sphere of our influence.

The virtue of justness is cultivated by seeking always to live according to our divine design. This means using the physical body to be productive and self-reliant, using our emotions and desires to express compassion and enthusiasm, using the mind to understand life, and using the will to enact the plans of our soul. The moment we let our personal will be dominated by irritability or stubborness, we cease to be just. The moment we let the emotions react in petty and personal ways, we fail the standard of justness. The moment we let our mind be flooded with doubt or pessimism, we likewise stop being just.

The great analog of justness is uprightness. The ability to "stand tall" has always been a symbol of justness. It represents the ideal of transcending the petty factors of daily life and responding only to the perfect design of the soul. Only an upright person can achieve this goal.

As we cultivate the virtue of justness, we come to realize that there is no room for relativism in our thinking. Divine intelligence has already created the ideal design for expressing ourselves physically, emotionally, and mentally. It is our job to discover this design and live up to it. Even debating whether or not such a design exists is a huge waste of time and energy.

We also come to be pervaded with a growing sense of correctness. We stop dealing with the results or effects of life—reacting to circumstances as they arise—and we begin dealing with causal forces. In other words, by treating others with goodwill and benevolence, we fill our lives with friends and associates we can rely upon. By expecting the best, we summon it to appear in our life—even if it is sometimes delayed in manifesting.

In understanding justness, however, it must be clearly seen that it is not the same as "fairness." We make a lot of fuss about fairness in society today, but very little of it is helpful. Under today's approach to fairness, Mt. Olympus should have been bulldozed so that all of the athletes at the Olympics would enjoy a "level playing field." The problem with this concept of fairness is that it is tied to the lowest common denominator within society—not to our divine design. It therefore intellectually traps us in materialism and illusion, rather than inspiring us with virtue.

Correctly understood, the virtue of justness explains why there is so much confusion today over the idea of moral goodness. When moral goodness is defined by what we dare not do, it ceases to be moral goodness and becomes the avoidance of moral badness. This leads to the common phenomenon of preachers exhorting their followers to avoid sin, which in turn offends many people at very deep levels.

Humanity has had just about all the sin it can absorb. Now we need something better. We need people who will act justly.

Temperance

Temperance is an idea in need of rehabilitation. It implies the ability to temper the blade of a sword in a forge, to give it strength. As such, it is the perfect model for self-discipline, as we temper our values, principles, and habits in the forge of our virtue, to give them greater strength and impact. Unfortunately, it has lately lost this meaning. Ever since the temperance movement, it has come to mean the forcible suppression of bad habits.

At its highest level, temperance is the process of flooding some aspect of our character with the light and love of the soul, to transform it into something more noble and helpful. We might recognize, for example, that we have a tendency to miss opportunities through laziness. Focusing on the habit of laziness, we would then think of the initiative of the soul flooding our character with a powerful level of motivation. In this way, we would temper our laziness with spiritual initiative.

A musician who wishes to perform with a greater level of virtuosity might also use temperance. Prior to beginning a performance, the musician would flood his or her own capacity for musical expressiveness with divine beauty and harmony. The result would be a higher, more sublime expression of musical genius.

In truth, there can be no virtue without temperance. Temperance embraces the entire process of self-discipline. It cleanses the vessel of our self-expression, so that divine currents can flow through us. It is what Franklin referred to as moderation; others might refer to it as restraint. It is not enough just to wish to be good and wise; it is not even enough to pray to be good and wise. We have to take whatever natural talent we have and carefully temper it with discipline, caution, and love.

A tree that grows in the wild will often be misshapen by wind and sun and other factors. But a tree that is trained properly from the time it is a seedling and pruned as necessary can become a thing of great beauty. In human life, temperance serves as the wise gardener who helps us grow into an expression of beauty, wisdom, and maturity.

We cultivate the virtue of temperance by becoming familiar with our habits, talents, and values, and then comparing them to the ideal design of divine life. Where they can be improved, we patiently flood them with the inner design, reinforcing their proper growth through our daily self-expression. As the virtue of temperance grows within our character in this manner, it subtly strengthens our whole demeanor in ways that cannot otherwise be achieved. We become more flexible, more tolerant, and more at peace with ourself.

Temperance is meant to be a personal interaction between the personality and the soul. In the instance of raising children, parents are meant to play the role of the soul in helping the child temper his or her character, until the child reaches maturity. In general, however, temperance is not a virtue we can impose on others. They must do their own work of self-discipline, in their own time. It is always important to respect the inner integrity of all people, and not try to coerce them into any kind of behavior, even if we firmly believe it to be in their own best interest.

Society, however, is a different matter, for each of us is an important component within society. It is right and proper to support the value of discipline throughout society, and insist on it in our primary institutions. It is a crime against temperance that our permissionary attitudes have gutted any real discipline in our public schools. The thought that education can occur in a disciplinary vacuum collapses under the weight of its own gross absurdity.

Confucius held that the best way to reform society is by reforming ourself first, then letting the virtue of our example spread through family, town, and state. He added, however, that a society can be no more virtuous than its leader. A leader, therefore—in any field—has an extra responsibility to demonstrate and teach virtue.

The loss of discipline throughout society has led to the marked increase in violence in our schools, the vast expansion of drug usage throughout our culture, and the rapid increase in hypocrisy in our elected officials. It has driven teenagers to rebel even more conspicuously than before, often to the point of violence. These trends are rapidly undermining the fabric of American life. Can they be reversed? Of course. What must we do?

First, restore self-discipline and temperance to their rightful places in social thinking.

Second, love virtue.

Integrity

One of the most popular concepts of contemporary philosophy has been deconstructionism, which basically states that there are no absolutes in life, and so the only way anything can have any meaning at all is by each one of us determining its importance to us. It has been this bizarre concept that has led to the complete breakdown of accuracy and reliability in journalism. Media doges have argued that since no journalist can know the absolute truth about any story, the reporter has a duty to "share" his or her personal opinions about it with the reader. There is, of course, no corresponding obligation to advise the reader that these "facts" are actually just opinions.

This kind of "thinking" is prevalent in society, and it endangers the core of wisdom and intelligence on which human civilization is based. The growth of the human race occurs as we achieve greater maturity. Any social tide that sweeps us back in the direction of immaturity is one that needs to be resisted—in the name of virtue.

When the Delphic oracle advised Athenians to "know thyself," it was never imagined that it would be interpreted as a command to embrace one's immaturity. Yet Americans by the millions are being cajoled to rediscover the child within them, as ested in igniting trouble than in solving problems, we are not acting with integrity.

As the virtue of integrity pervades our awareness, it helps us integrate conflicting issues that may still exist within us, and eliminate hypocrisy. It opens our eyes so that we can truly see who we are.

At last, we come to know ourself—and what it means to be true.

Beauty

The process of human growth is a long saga of refinement. This is perhaps most clearly seen in the context of society. Civilization grows as we refine our manners, customs, tastes, national habits, and ethics. Gradually, we elevate all of these aspects of human life, so that they embody more and more of the virtues of divine life.

Perhaps the best symbol of this refinement is beauty. Almost every human being is preoccupied with beauty—even though our interest tends to be focused mostly in physical appearances. We see beauty as a key to success. We therefore spend amazing amounts of time and money investing in our personal expression of beauty. Some of us even become obsessed by it.

While obsession is never healthy, our absorption with beauty does illustrate the power of virtue in our lives, even if misapplied. We know there is an inner mystery to beauty, and so we strive after it, even though we may never attain it. In the process, we learn to refine ourselves.

To tap the inner essence of beauty, of course, we must do more than buy creams and powders and apply them daily. We must seek out and destroy any tendencies toward ugliness in our consciousness, and strive mightily to replace them with issues of beauty. We need to begin to resonate in response to divine beauty. We must also discredit the notion that "beauty is in the eye of the beholder," a concept that reeks of relativistic thinking. Being a divine force, beauty is an absolute. It can be known. We can fill our whole awareness with the virtue of beauty. We can express it.

Divine life expresses beauty through its principles and proportions. The inner essence of great music is a radiant display of beauty. So is the power with which an angel nourishes life in a fertile valley, or across a whole mountain range. There is beauty within every legitimate creative inspiration—and every new scientific discovery as well. There is beauty in the heart of a mature, enlightened person.

Our job is to harness this beauty to eradicate ugliness and crudeness, not in physical appearance (which is adjudged largely on the basis of custom), but in physical action. Cruelty toward others and animals is ugly. Child abuse is barbaric. Drunkenness is crude. Self-pity is ugly. Bitterness is vulgar. Pessimism is crude. Conflict is barbaric.

There is plenty of ugliness on a larger scale as well. Horror movies are deliberately crude. Rap music and hard rock are barbaric. A large chunk of modern dance and art is ugly, especially when the artist or dancer is trying to capture feelings of alienation, sorrow, or guilt. Racism is obscene. Victimhood is vulgar. Welfare enslavement is barbaric.

The only force that can redeem ugliness is the virtue of beauty, beauty drawn from the divine fountain of cleansing water in the heart of the garden of Eden (the level of spirit). The love of beauty lifts us steadily toward a stronger and fuller identification with divine beauty. As we interact with this divine beauty, it refines our understanding so that we can begin to perceive more and more subtle levels of beauty. Our tastes become more sublime. Our ability to grasp subtleties expands. We start working more and more consciously at abstract levels of realization.

This is the power of the virtue of beauty: it lifts us into the abstract, even while we are alive in the concrete. It transforms our comprehension of living. It brings into our life a will and a power that cannot be attained in any other way: the will to add to the glory of the Father.

Patience

The great Spanish mystic, St. Teresa de Avila, put it succintly: *"Con la paciencia, todo alcanza."* With patience, everything can be realized. One of the great sources of stress in our modern age is impatience. We build unrealistic expectations about rapid growth and instant change, and then are disappointed when results come slowly. We seek short cuts, and are discouraged when they turn out to be dead ends. We try to ram our way through projects and activities, instead of adopting a reasonable, rhythmic pace more in harmony with the work to be done.

We need to pause from time to time and recollect that God has set aside millions of years for this present phase of evolution. There is no expectation in heaven that perfection will be achieved on earth by next Tuesday—or even by the year 3000! When we start complaining about how slow human growth is, we are generating a silly side-issue. It is not our duty to alter the divine rhythm! It is our duty to seize the opportunities that come to us to be a better person.

Patience recognizes that opportunity and difficulty are two sides of the same coin, and that both arrive as a single package in our lives. We may feel thwarted by circumstances today, but that is no reason for taking rash action. If we wait patiently for the right moment to act, we should be able to seize the winds of opportunity to fill our sails, rather than having to try to tack into a gale.

By cultivating the virtue of patience, we connect ourselves with the divine quality of peace—the ability to work with serenity in the midst of chaos and opposition. We become aware of the pace the soul is setting for us in our life, and are flooded by its rhythm. As a result, we will seem to have a growing talent for controlling circumstances and always acting at the right moment. In fact, this is the creative expression of patience.

The need for patience in society is made poignantly clear in the realm of politics. Everybody in America who discovers something wrong or unfair about life in this nation seems to believe that it must be corrected immediately. So we rush to pass laws that will prevent the unjustness from ever occurring again, only to find that the "solution" is often worse than the original problem.

The price of impatience is a loss of historical perspective. With all of the stress and demands of modern life, who has time to read history? By and large, we have become a nation of voters who have no concept of history at all. As a result, we have no extensive time frame in which to bracket our thoughts. Our understanding of current problems is limited to this moment of time—a certain recipe for disaster.

Let us take a lesson from the process of birth. A baby is not born a day or a week after conception. It requires nine months on the average for a healthy baby to develop. Nor does an infant become a mature adult in a month. It requires roughly twenty years for a child to grow into adulthood—and often a good many more years for the adult to become mature. Patience is required.

Just so, everything worthwhile that we may do requires a time for gestation. A book does not leap into existence the moment it is first conceived. The idea must sit on the shelf of possibilities for a while. Then it must be shaped into an outline and put back on the shelf for another while. During this time, the concept develops and expands at unconscious levels. When the book is finally ready to be written, the author is alerted to this state of readiness by being flooded by a compelling motive to write.

This same pattern should be used in developing new businesses, raising a family, instituting new social policies, or approaching any other creative work. It is a mistake to start acting prematurely. We need to act instead with patience.

Then we can act with virtue.

Integrating Virtue

It is not just enough to know about virtue, of course; the important thing is to start to act with virtue. This requires a long process of integrating the virtues of divine life into our character and behavior—a process which begins with self-examination and culminates with active interaction with the spiritual qualities of living. It is a process of continual revision and refocusing, as we refine our understanding of these most sublime guidelines to human excellence.

In addition to learning to think for ourself, as has already been described, there are several ways we can enrich the work of learning to love virtue. These are all tried and true methods that have been known to humanity for thousands of years, but are still not used by most human beings on a regular basis. They are all designed to help us learn to interact more effectively with the divine qualities that inspire virtue.

The first practice is **faith.** This is not just belief in God, as many people assume. Faith is the ability to focus our expectations on our goal, whatever that may be. Many people abuse this power by investing faith in their imminent failure or destruction. Intelligent people, however, have learned that a strong measure of faith is the easiest and most direct way to open our mind and heart to the reality of divine life within us. In this way, we use faith to build a strong bridge to the source of virtue.

The second practice is **acting as if.** Bogged down in conflict and stress, we may not feel as if we have any connection with harmony. But harmony does exist in the highest realms of our being, as an attribute of spirit. So, even though we may feel bereft and confused, we try to act as if we were an agent of harmony—indeed, a perfect expression of harmony and concord. In this way, we invoke the harmony within our spirit, and it pours into our awareness. Suddenly, we realize that we had more potential for harmony than we ever realized!

The third practice is **gratitude.** We need to build a strong bridge with the spiritual forces within us. Faith opens the gate; acting as if we had these qualities induces an outpouring of them. But we need more than just an occasional trickle. We need a steady, reliable inflow of each of these virtues. This is where the practice of gratitude sparkles—not because the soul vainly needs our thankfulness, but because the personality needs to be trained in the spiritual art of recollection or remembrance. When confronted by temptation, it must be able to recollect the strong presence of temperance. When confronted by ugliness, it must be able to remember the abiding presence of beauty. Such recollection can only occur if the personality has built up a strong awareness of the inner proximity of these forces. As we express gratitude and thankfulness for these virtues, this bridge is constructed.

This gratitude must not be pro forma, however—a ritual to be raced through every night before we fall asleep. Ideally, we will pause regularly throughout the day to express our thanks for the virtues which have already blossomed in our character. When we make an intelligent decision, therefore, we should give thanks for the presence of justness and wisdom. When we help another person, we should give thanks for our goodwill. When we have the strength to wait for the right moment to act, we should express gratitude for the virtue of patience. Even if we occasionally fall short of expressing the ideal, we should give thanks that we are in the process of learning to do better.

The practice of gratitude in this fashion is both simple and powerful. Our gratitude links us dynamically to the will of God, so that we contact not just the appearance of virtue, but also its seminal nature—its capacity to grow and mature within our character. Gratitude links us with the motivating force of virtue, thereby accelerating the process of becoming a *virtuosi* immensely.

Finally, the fourth step is **blessing.** Virtue develops as we blend the best within us with divine life.

As we become schooled in virtue, we become much more sensitive to the best within others, society, and all of life. It is therefore important to share our virtue with others on a regular basis. Eventually, this should become the active expression of virtue in all that we do. But no one can be expected to start behaving with virtue overnight. So, while we are still developing this rich inner presence, we can practice the expression of virtue by cultivating the habit of blessing others, society, and life.

The act of blessing is described in full in the essay "Finding Meaning in Life" in the first volume of *The Art of Living*. It is not especially religious in nature, although it can have a spiritual application. It is the simple act of focusing the best within ourself to draw forth and strengthen the best within others, our country, or our civilization. A parent, for example, could bless the emerging maturity within his or her child. A citizen could bless the capacity of all citizens to honor and support the ideal of freedom.

We can use the act of blessing to focus the divine life within any virtue into our own life and work, for the benefit of others, or for society as a whole. The repeated practice of blessing helps us develop basic skills in expressing these virtues as an integral part of our character. It grounds the divine—through our own life.

A Call for Virtue

To be effective, the work of cultivating virtue—through the process already described—should be combined with an effort to learn as much about virtue as possible. Not too many years ago, this learning would have been automatic, as we became educated in the classics and other ancient writings. But since the turn of the century, these teachings have been steadily de-emphasized in American public education—and we all have been impoverished mentally as a consequence.

The damage can be repaired, however. We can educate ourselves in the meaning and value of virtue. This process involves reading many of the books already cited in this treatise, but it extends far beyond reading alone. Society is no longer nurtured by books alone; we draw many of our key ideas from other sources. Certainly, television, popular music, and films—and now the Internet—are far more direct influences on the values and ethics of the newest generations than books. We must therefore learn how important it is to listen and respond to these influences with enlightened discrimination.

In an age corrupted by the incessant presence of rock music, the person of virtue needs to recognize that most rock music is devoid of virtue. The lyrics often trap us in violence and rebellion; the music is primitive, dissonant, and jarring. There is no sign that any of this music has ever been inspired by spiritual levels. It is therefore necessary to nourish our need for music with something that has been inspired by spirit. The works of Bach, Beethoven, Mozart, Handel, and Wagner, among others, connect us very quickly with divine realms when we listen to them perceptively. They draw in angelic forces which revel in the music. This music stimulates whatever virtue we have cultivated in our own life, and strengthens it.

Modern movies also present the need for discrimination. Films from the first half of the twentieth century usually tried to inspire the audience with one virtue or another: courage, goodwill, or integrity. Some modern movies do as well. But many seem intent on exploring only the ugly, dark, and violent side of human nature. They glorify immaturity; they wallow in stupidity, viciousness, and discontent. In some cases, they deliberately try to induce terror and shock. The person of virtue will stay away from such movies—or, if drawn into seeing one unaware of the actual content—will get up and walk out of the showing. The price we pay by exposing our subconscious to such garbage is simply too high.

This is not a call for censorship; it is a call for virtue. There is no reason to ask the law to regulate movies or music; the choice not to watch or listen is the responsibility of the intelligent adult. Intelligent people will nourish their mental pantry shelves with movies and music and books which educate and elevate.

The same guidelines apply to the fine arts. A painting of great mastery can directly stimulate the virtue of beauty, among others. But a painting of anger or depression will sound the wrong keynote in our consciousness. It will drag us down, not lift us up.

In this regard, it should be noted that there is nothing unvirtuous or immoral about the presence of nudity in good art, unless the nudity is used as an adjunct to sadism or degradation. Nudity is a symbol for truth, and was often used during the Renaissance in the portrayal of virtue, as well as in highly spiritual allegories. The condemnation of nudity as immoral is a sign of smallmindedness, not virtue.

In a broader sense, we must exercise the same measure of discrimination in choosing all of our experiences in life. Gossip may seem to many people to be a harmless pastime, but it focuses the mind into triviality and pettiness. It therefore robs our attentiveness of energy that could otherwise be spent on cultivating virtue.

In general, it is difficult to cultivate virtue if we allow our consciousness to be divided, spending part of our time acquiring virtue while simultaneously devoting the rest of it to activities that are devoid of virtue. An example of this contradiction lies in our modern schools. Until this century, schools were devoted to education. At the start of this century, however, schools began to add other functions of a non-educational nature. One of the major ones is athletics. Today, almost every school and college competes with other schools and colleges in football, basketball, baseball, and many other sports. At first, these activities were "tacked on" to the school's agenda. Today, however, it is unthinkable to build a school without a massive athletic complex, including a gymnasium that can seat hundreds of fans. All of this is routinely included in the cost of educating our youth. But do sports serve true educational goals? They are fun, of course—but do they help students cultivate their inner talents and character? Until twenty-five years ago, the answer was automatic: of course they do. They promote sportsmanship, and sportsmanship embodies all kinds of virtue. In the last few years, though, it has become abundantly clear that athletic programs do not promote sportsmanship; they promote conflict. They may well be a factor in the increasingly violent climate in schools.

If athletics actually drain off money that could be more constructively used to fund education, then what is their justification? Why not conduct athletic competitions between town and town, rather than school and school? This may not seem to be a major issue confronting modern society, but it is more significant than it seems. Modern education is faltering. It has lost much of its virtue. In trying to understand how this has happened, it is important to make sure we consider all possible factors.

Herein lies an illustration of the work of cultivating virtue. Society wants good education, but it also wants to identify with "school spirit." It has no idea how much the presence of competitive athletic programs erodes the quality of education. It has no idea how much a lax attitude toward discipline encourages drugs, alcohol abuse, and violence. As a consequence, these conflicting forces are present in every public school system in the United States. We cannot put virtue back into education until we resolve these conflicts.

Similar conflicts about values and ethics may also occur within our personal psychology, making it difficult for virtue to take root. If we cling to outdated religious attitudes about worthlessness and sin, these beliefs can generate a tremendous conflict in trying to cultivate a proper sense of reverence—that we are a son or daughter of God possessing, deep within ourself, a birthright of virtue. In order to cultivate a greater measure of virtue, therefore, we must identify these areas of conflict and correct them in a way that honors our highest values and beliefs.

The bottom line is simple. To become a person of virtue, we must put most of our time and energy into activities that can help us cultivate our spiritual self-expression. Part of this process involves deciding not to put so much effort into activities that are counterproductive.

There is no idea so sacred that it cannot stand up to this kind of evaluation. To cultivate virtue, we must be willing to hold up to the light of scrutiny every taboo that we are not allowed to talk about in school, on television, or in polite society. We must think, and then act accordingly.

Contacting Virtue

If we are serious about cultivating virtue, however, there is only so much that we can do by reading, reflecting, and praying. At some point, we must learn to work directly with the transcendent levels of virtue—the link that joins a human value or principle with a divine ideal, and makes it a virtue.

Socrates taught that the key to working with virtue was to train the mind to work directly with the level of Forms—the divine blueprint for acting and thinking in any facet of life. These Forms are the abstract essence of human values—the inner essence of courage, faith, honesty, or discipline.

St. Francis de Sales described the process of training the mind to work in this way as meditation. In his *Introduction to the Devout Life,* he wrote: "By often turning your eyes on God in meditation, your whole soul will be filled with the light of the world." In this way, we will be able to see the difference between the mundane interpretation of a value or principle and the divine reality behind it.

Such meditation must be active, rather than passive. It is not enough just to be still and wait for the dove of the Holy Spirit to descend and anoint us with wisdom. We must focus our thoughts and attention on one of the virtues of life, and then ask for intuitive guidance in understanding the ideal divine plan for expressing this virtue in our own life. We must consider what habits and priorities need to be changed in our daily behavior to make room for this value, and we must also try to sense the inflowing power of virtue itself, lifting us to a higher level of comprehension.

A meditation on virtue can follow a simple format:

1. Relax the body.

2. Rise above any discomfort or anxiety in the emotions or the mind.

3. Recollect your inner connection with divine life. If you have meditated before, recall the highest level of contact you have earlier attained.

4. Choose a virtue to cultivate meditatively—for example, goodwill. (Like Franklin, you might wish to work with a different one each week.)

5. Review your own attitudes and values concerning this virtue. How effectively do you express it? Where is there room for improvement? What habits or attitudes interfere with expressing goodwill?

6. Think of the divine pattern for goodwill as being a point of light a few inches above the top of your head. Imagine this point being connected, as a triangle, with a second point of light directly in front of your forehead, plus a third point of light just behind the throat.

7. Imagine the power of the virtue of divine goodwill flowing through this triangle, awakening a stronger awareness of the divine design for expressing goodwill in the point of light in front of your forehead. At the same time, it also awakens your capacity to act with virtue in the point behind the throat.

8. Once this circulation is established, let the ideal plan for this virtue direct your thoughts and contemplations, as you strive to understand the higher nature of goodwill.

9. Register this virtue as clearly as you can in your own attitudes and beliefs. The work of registering the power of a virtue should crescendo to a complete expression of love for the virtue at the end of the meditation.

This meditation can be made even more effective by thinking of the point of light a foot above the head as a radiant jewel. This is the source of virtue within us. The point of light just in front of the forehead can be thought of as an altar—the altar of our character in which virtue interacts with our habits and attitudes to guide and discipline us. The third point, behind the throat, can be thought of as a chalice, which, as it is filled with virtue, spills over into our daily self-expression.

As contact is made via the triangle, it becomes an avenue for the flow of the divine virtue of goodwill into our awareness and consciousness. It should be thought of as an ongoing flow of energy throughout our consciousness. (The energy that flows from the chalice to the jewel is, of course, the energy of our own devotion and invocation.)

The symbolism in this meditation was inspired by a passage in Dante's *The Divine Comedy:*

> This precious jewel
> In which every virtue has its basis,
> How did it come to you?

The altar reminds us of our need to sacrifice the nonvirtuous elements of our character in order to create virtue; the chalice reminds us that we must act with virtue in all that we do.

This brief meditative exercise, when repeated regularly, will help us explore and cultivate the divine design for any virtue—plus help us integrate the power of virtue into our own awareness.

As a result, virtue becomes a divine reality that we can experience for ourself every day of our life. Once we have contacted virtue in this way and have integrated it into our self-expression, we know it is a powerful force that is always present in our life.

It can be relied upon.

It is a source of strength that links us always to God.

Teaching Virtue to Children

Virtue is a blend of the best within our personality with the spiritual qualities of divine life. As such, no human being enters physical life with a fully developed sense of virtue. Some may have a natural affinity toward the life of spirit, but no child has any practical experience in cultivating virtue. Each must learn it on his or her own, either during childhood or, with more difficultly, as an adult.

Teaching virtue is the responsibility of a child's parents, as they serve as surrogates for the child's soul. In an enlightened society, there would be many sources of help for parents. In ours, there are just a few, and many of these are unreliable.

The major groundwork for cultivating virtue must be laid in the home life, by the example of the parents. In addition, the Sunday School teachings that can be found in most churches and temples today can be helpful in reinforcing what parents teach. A basic exposure to the ethics and values of any major religion can provide a solid base upon which the parents can build. Nonetheless, parents must still exert supervision. Sunday School teachers can be full of nonsense as well as helpful guidance. If a teacher starts frightening children with stories of sinfulness and eternal suffering, it is time to take them elsewhere.

Scouting programs for both boys and girls can also provide an excellent basis for cultivating virtue, teaching the gamut from trustworthiness to reverence. But care must be taken that scout programs do not become militaristic or materialistic.

Public schools are no longer a reliable source of education in the virtues. Instead of the golden rule, children are more apt to be taught that environmental terrorism is good, because it stands up to the willful violence of "unprincipled corporations." Instead of the pledge of allegiance, they are more apt to be taught the use of condoms.

It is therefore important for parents to make a deliberate effort to supply the instruction on virtue that is now notably absent in our schools. This effort begins, of course, with the realization that the best tool for teaching virtue to children is to set a good example. Children mimic the example of their parents, and yearn to do grown-up things, so that they will be recognized as an adult, too. All too often, however, the chief objects of this yearning are driving a car, drinking alcohol, taking drugs, and being in control of their own life. The reason why is simple. These are all things that adults can do that children cannot.

Ideally, parental instruction in virtue would reverse this scenario, and children would grow up yearning to be able to express goodwill, courage, and wisdom in adult ways. They would know the value of being cheerful and acting with integrity and patience in all situations.

How can this be achieved? Parents must begin setting the tone early in childhood. Just as there are principles we must follow in life, there should be clear principles of behavior and conduct within each family. These principles should be enunciated and explained by the parents, and there should be appropriate reinforcements of them.

Parents are also responsible for making sure their children are appropriately nourished, both mentally and emotionally. Most parents would consider themselves derelict if they allowed their children to live exclusively on Twinkies.® A parallel approach should be taken in monitoring the attitudes and ideas that children consume. Do video games foster virtue? Most of them seem to promote violence, rudeness, and rebellion. It does not make sense to allow children to be exposed to such recreation. At the same time, however, it may not be useful to prohibit such games. It is far better to explain why they are harmful, and encourage children to cooperate voluntarily. It is also important to channel their youthful energy into more constructive activities.

Much of the work of helping children to cultivate virtue can be accomplished by guiding them carefully as they learn to read. Many of the stories William Bennett has compiled in his *Book of Virtues* are quite helpful in this way. In addition, there are many other sources of inspiration for values. Children have active imaginations, and these imaginations are waiting to be nourished. Allegories, fables, and myths stimulate the imagination while teaching solid principles of virtue.

As children become teenagers, they begin to deal with the realm of ethics and ideas. They need strong models for excellence, courage, faith, and temperance. In particular, they need to be taught the virtue of courage, so they will have the strength to stand up to peer pressure, and teenage fads. They need to be taught that they can think for themselves—and encouraged to do so.

Teenagers are also nearing the point where they must start the work of cultivating virtue for themselves. For this reason, the work of teaching virtue must be less didactic and more supportive. If a child insists on listening to rock music, there is no point in creating a conflict over this choice. A more enlightened response is to ask the child to listen to it in his own room, without disturbing the rest of the household, and to explain the harm he may be doing to his consciousness—and eardrums.

Clearly, the work of teaching virtue to children should never be approached as a pitched battle between the generations. We need only to remember that harmony is a virtue—and discord is not. To disrupt an entire household by militantly trying to enforce the principles of virtue is itself an assault on virtue! As always, common sense and pragmatism are the best safeguards.

The fact that children will be interacting with other children, who may not have the same foundation in virtue, underscores the need to be flexible. Parents ought to explain lucidly why other families might teach or emphasize other values or interpretations of the virtues. Once again, it is helpful to remember that tolerance is an important facet of the virtue of goodwill.

Most children crave guidelines to help them live their lives more successfully. It is therefore reasonably easy to teach a child that God has designed human beings to act in certain ways. Many adults have not yet learned to behave in these ideal ways, and so they act in whatever way seems most immediately rewarding. This is generally not a good way to act, however. Cheating makes other people mad. Cowardice makes it difficult to accomplish anything. Depression drives other people away. To the best of our ability, therefore, we ought to try to understand this divine design and live up to it. In truth, this inner design is within us, helping us whenever we pause to listen to it.

Children also need to learn that virtue is something each of us must build for ourself. It is not right to try to force virtue or morality on anyone else. If people ask for our advice, we should offer it. But otherwise, we must learn to respect other people and not try to tell them how to live.

As children mature, it is important for parents to help them develop the wisdom to think for themselves and the courage to defend their principles. It is therefore important to discuss the hidden messages within a political speech or an advertisement seen on television. Parents should encourage their children, especially teenagers, to initiate conversations and questions about ethics, conflicts, and current events. As much as possible, these sessions should inspire the child to discover the inner nature of virtue on his or her own.

The work of teaching virtue to children is a project that begins in the cradle and is not complete until adulthood. Nonetheless, it is important for parents to understand that once their children have become adults, they cease to be children. They may still be offspring, but they have left the nest. It is vitally important, therefore, to treat them like adults—and stop trying to parent them.

One more point needs to be made in this regard. Parents should not overlook the capacity of a child to teach its parents about their own shortcomings concerning virtue. Wherever conflict arises between parent and child, it emphasizes not only an area of immaturity in the child but likewise an area of immaturity in the parent. The wise parent will seize this conflict as an opportunity to glean new insight into one of his or her weak spots.

Restoring Virtue in Society

Virtue is our link to God. From it, we develop a set of values and principles called ethics, which guide us in our daily affairs. But virtue is not just a set of intellectual concepts. Each virtue contains the vital power of divine life. Virtue can therefore be developed only within ourselves.

For this reason, it is important never to think that we are called to enforce virtue on others. It cannot be done. The Catholic church tried and failed in the Inquisition. The United States government tried and failed with Prohibition. God does not ask us to force other people to be virtuous. It is enough to learn how to express virtue in our own life.

Nonetheless, we do have an obligation to help virtue grow within society. As a part of society, we have a legitimate interest in helping society learn to love virtue. We should certainly be a voice for virtue in public discussions of issues. But once we have made our voice heard, we should go no further. We should respect the will of the whole, even if we disagree with it. After all, integrity is a virtue.

Herein lie some of the roots of much of our modern social turmoil. In a society of recognized virtue, it was considered wise to address the errors within society through self-reform. This method was espoused, for example, by Booker T. Washington, the great black educator and leader. He advised blacks to press for equality by "reinventing" themselves through education and integrating themselves into American culture. This approach—which mirrors the teachings of Confucius on how to increase virtue in society—fell out of favor with blacks and other minority groups in the twentieth century. They pressed for reforms in society more vigorously. While it managed to provoke legal reforms, it has failed to solve the underlying problems. In many ways, in fact, it has exacerbated the tensions and gaps within society, thereby setting the stage for violence.

Violence, it should be noted, is generally a clear sign of the need for renewed virtue.

The problems of today, in fact, can be traced directly to the protests and demonstrations of the 1960s. Through the medium of protest, even nonviolent protest, the push for reform was rocketed forward. Virtue, unfortunately, was left behind.

Is all protest nonvirtuous? Of course not. But true reform is an expression of divine goodwill. Divine goodwill cannot be expressed except within the context of the deepest, most loving respect for others—including those in power. This was not a characteristic of the protest movement of the 1960s, which was, in truth, little more than rabble-rousing. It was motivated by the urge to destroy, rather than the need for reform.

We are still reaping the whirlwind generated by the seeds of discontent "blowing in the wind" of the 1960s. Only a new wave of virtue throughout our society can reverse these lamentable trends.

In general, American society needs to recognize the value of preserving the virtue with which it has been blessed. The fanatical blindness with which many Americans have pursued the separation of church and state over the past one hundred years, for example, is appalling. The Bill of Rights directs the government not to infringe upon the freedom of churches to establish themselves in this country; it does not tell the government to divorce itself from God! Such an idea would be horrific to Washington, Jefferson, and Franklin. They knew that the country was founded on virtue, and depended upon virtue to survive.

There has clearly been a loss of virtue in our society over the past one hundred and fifty years. But this is no cause for discouragement. Virtue is still alive and active at the inner realms of human living. It is gently, subtly encouraging society to rediscover the power of virtue—not as a sense of moral goodness to be imposed on everyone, but as the presence of God, alive within our minds and hearts.

With any luck, we may be able to leave both the Permissionaries and the Prohibitionists behind as we embrace a new understanding of virtue for the third millenium. No matter how blind humanity may seem to be at the moment, this ignorance shall pass. There will be a reawakening to divine guidance and design.

Virtue shall prevail.

The Legacy of Virtue

We need to remember that virtue operates at unconscious, abstract levels. Virtue is our connection with God, our link to the soul. The thinking and reflecting we do about virtue is conscious, of course, but the living vitality of virtue derives from the divine design. This living force is therefore at work influencing and directing society, even when society seems to ignore virtue and its power. It is also at work guiding us individually, even if we are unaware of it.

While virtue exists at inner, invisible dimensions of life, it is not by any means imaginary. Wherever a person of virtue lives and works, an accumulation of virtue occurs. Many of the Catholic shrines throughout the world are repositories of great virtue, especially if they commemorate the home or workplace of a saint. Relics of saints likewise carry a potent charge of virtue. The same is often true of Hindu and Buddhist shrines in the East.

In this country, there is a notable focus of virtue at the Mt. Washington United Methodist Church in Baltimore, Maryland, where healing services have been conducted every Thursday morning for almost fifty years. The process of genuine spiritual healing automatically brings in a tremendous force of virtue. Most of it is transferred to the people seeking healing, but a strong residue of virtue remains permanently in the church as well.

This is not to say that all churches and temples are repositories of virtue. Even if they have been sanctified, they are not automatically filled with virtue. It would take the ongoing presence of a person or group of substantial virtue to leave such a lasting legacy.

One does not have to be a saint to be a person of virtue, of course. Among the founding fathers, George Washington, Benjamin Franklin, and Thomas Jefferson all exuded virtue. In them, virtue was heavily blended with the spirit of America and the divine ideals of freedom and liberty. It is possible to be directly inspired by this virtue by visiting their homes and workplaces.

Part of our design, as human beings, is to build up such a strong charge of virtue in our presence that we do leave behind a residue of virtue that elevates the very substance we touch. It is a powerful way that we are able to bring heaven to earth—and leave it for posterity.

The virtue we leave behind, after all, is immortal.

A Person of Virtue

It is not enough to turn our life over to God. The Creator wants us to develop our own intelligence, will, and motivation. God wants us to live up to His Image on earth, carrying out His plans and implementing His will.

To be a person of virtue, therefore, we must do more than believe in virtue. We must do more than study virtue.

We must love virtue.

What does this mean?

Love is the great attractive energy of life. We can become aware of virtue through our studies, but we can build a link with God's image only through love.

We must love the perfect design of God and strive always to express it in our daily lives, to the best of our comprehension.

We must hold our minds and hearts steady in the inflowing power of virtue, so that it may saturate our whole being.

We must respect all other human beings, understanding that they are designed to become people of virtue every bit as much as we. We must never let virtue divide us from others, or make us feel superior to them. We are all brothers in the family of God—regardless of our gender—and we should treat one another as such. How can we possibly know virtue or love virtue if we fail to respect the God within all people, regardless of their beliefs, their nationality, their ethnic heritage, or their character?

To love virtue, we must open our minds to be responsive to God.

To love virtue, we must open our hearts to the best within ourself—and within all other people, all life forms.

To love virtue, we must align our personal motivations with the spiritual will of the soul.

To love virtue, we must love excellence and promote it whenever and wherever we can.

To love virtue, we must love society and seek to make civilization as great as possible.

To love virtue, we must bring heaven to earth.

To love virtue, we must find the image of God imprinted deep within our being, magnify it, and give birth to it in our daily life, so that all may see.

By loving virtue, we know God. We are able, at last, to do God's will.

A Collect on Virtue

Love virtue!
Open your mind
    and direct your thoughts toward God.
Seek God within the sanctuary of your heart.
Let God appear before you,
As the compelling breath of virtue.
Trust in His divine love, power, and wisdom.

Virtue leads us to God,
It links us to His will.
Virtue is the image of God,
Imprinted in our soul at the dawn of creation.
Virtue is our birthright.
Only a fool would barter it away.

To love virtue,
We must approach the altar of God
Willing to sacrifice those shortcomings
    which cause us to stumble and fall,
So that we may be purified and transformed
In the steady light of goodness.

It is not possible to have virtue
    Unless we know God.
It is not possible to honor virtue
    Unless we love God.

Therefore, we call upon the presence of God
    within us
To sanctify the noble qualities and talents
That we have already forged within the
    furnace of our character,
And reveal to us the jewel of virtue
Taking shape in our own life.

Like the breath of God,
Virtue is born of spirit.
It flows into our awareness
And fills our mind and heart
As we create the chalice that will receive it.
We can then be reborn from above.

As virtue overflows the chalice
Of our goodwill and devotion
It cleanses us of the impurities
Of thought and feeling and habit
That fail to honor the highest.
We build new virtue
So that we can more perfectly express
    the image of God
Through everything we do.

The person of virtue has everything
And lacks nothing.
Let us therefore seek our fulfillment in virtue.

Let divine love cleanse the heart.
Let divine wisdom inspire the mind.
Let divine strength renew the body.
And let our acts be impelled by the will of God.

May virtue saturate the heart.
May virtue penetrate the mind.
May virtue direct our actions.

Love virtue,
For as we love virtue,
We love God and know God,
And fulfill His love for us.

Recommended Reading

The work of cultivating virtue is best supported by an active program of reading. A lot has been written over the years about virtue, and much of it is helpful. Here are a few places to begin:

• The dialogues of Plato, especially *Meno, Protogoras, The Republic,* and *Crito.*

• *The Bhagavad-Gita.*

• *The Tao Te Ching,* by Lao Tsu.

• *I Ching on Line,* a set of four books about the use of the I Ching to build a structure of practical philosophy, by Robert R. Leichtman, M.D. and Carl Japikse.

• "The Wisdom of Solomon" in *The Bible.* (One edition that includes this book is *The Jerusalem Bible.)*

• "The Gospel of Matthew" in *The Bible.*

• *Introduction to the Devout Life,* by St. Francis de Sales.

• *The Prince,* by Niccolo Machiavelli.

- *Common Sense,* by Thomas Paine.

- *The Autobiography of Benjamin Franklin.*

- *An Essay on Man* plus *The Moral Essays,* by Alexander Pope.

- The essays of Ralph Waldo Emerson.

- The essays of Sir Francis Bacon.

- The stories of Nathaniel Hawthorne.

- *The Art of Living,* five volumes of essays by Robert R. Leichtman, M.D. and Carl Japikse. This set of books contains complete descriptions of many of the virtues listed in this book, plus others.

- *The Life of Spirit,* five volumes of essays by Robert R. Leichtman, M.D. and Carl Japikse. These essays examine the nature of spirit and methods for integrating spirit into our daily lives.

- *The Book of Virtues,* by William Bennett.

For help in ordering any of these books, check out Ariel Press's website at www.stc.net/~light, or call 1-800-336-7769 Monday through Friday.

Ordering More Copies

Additional copies of *Love Virtue* may be purchased at any bookstore, on the internet, or directly from the publisher. Single copies cost $9.99 plus $4 shipping for one book, $6 for two or more books. Ten or more copies sent to one address cost $8 each plus $8 shipping. Twenty-five copies or more to one address cost $6 each plus $10 shipping.

To order, send a check or money order to Ariel Press, P.O. Box 297, Marble Hill, GA 30148. Or call toll free 1 (800) 336-7769 weekdays and charge the order to MasterCard, VISA, Diners, American Express, or Discover.

Ariel Press publishes many other fine books as well. Our entire catalog can be accessed at no charge on the internet at www.stc.net/~light, or a copy can be bought for $6 directly from the publisher. The catalog is sent free with orders of $15 or more. It contains a coupon for $10 off on a subsequent purchase.

Ariel Press is the publishing house of Light, a nonprofit charitable organization dedicated to enriching human understanding of spirit and creativity. We welcome your support. All donations to Light are tax deductible and help us pursue our charitable goals. For further information, please call 1-800-336-7769.